ENCOUNTERS IN MY TRAVELS
THOUGHTS ALONG THE WAY

VIBS

Volume 174

Robert Ginsberg
Founding Editor

Peter A. Redpath
Executive Editor

Associate Editors

a volume in
Lived Values: Valued Lives
LVVL
Richard T. Hull, Editor

ENCOUNTERS IN MY TRAVELS
THOUGHTS ALONG THE WAY

Dixie Lee Harris

Rodopi

Amsterdam - New York, NY 2006

Cover Design: Studio Pollmann

The paper on which this book is printed meets the requirements of "ISO 9706:1994, Information and documentation - Paper for documents - Requirements for permanence".

ISBN: 90-420-1788-0
©Editions Rodopi B.V., Amsterdam - New York, NY 2006
Printed in the Netherlands

CONTENTS

Foreword   vii

Introduction   1

ONE   Police Encounters   3

TWO   Alaska, 1957–1960   31

THREE   Roads Traveled   43

FOUR   War!   67

FIVE   In the Muslim World   75

SIX   Natural Wonders   87

SEVEN   Built Wonders   97

EIGHT   Other Encounters   117

NINE   Epilogue   127

For Further Reading   131

About the Author   133

Index   135

FOREWORD

I first met Dixie Lee Harris as a student in a course in critical thinking I was teaching at the Center for Inquiry Transnational in Amherst, New York. It was an interesting class comprised of students from college undergraduates to octogenarians, with even a classics professor and a Nobel Prize nominee tossed in. Dixie Lee impressed me by her contrast with the more garrulous members of the class: She was quiet, attentive, and watchful, but did not speak up much.

I saw her at several other Center events, most recently a year ago in Toronto, Canada. There I made so bold as to speak with her, and she gradually opened up about herself. I had just successfully proposed this series, Lived Values, Valued Lives (LVVL), to the Value Inquiry Books Series editors and was looking for titles. Dixie Lee mentioned that she had a manuscript about her travels around the world, and I said I thought it might fit into my new series.

I found Dixie Lee Harris's adventures to be fascinating in a variety of ways. She demonstrates that extensive travel is possible without incurring great expense is instructive. Her experiences have been much closer to the lives of the common folk of the countries she has visited than the typical tourist fare. Her encounters are eye opening even to one who has traveled a fair amount.

The Lived Values, Valued Lives Series is comprised of biographies, loosely defined, that express and explore how values appear in, and shape, human lives. We intend to provoke readers to engage in reflective exploration of values expressed in the decisions, actions, and thoughts of philosophically reflective individuals. From one another's narratives we can learn much and come to consider possibilities that might otherwise never occur to us.

Dixie Lee Harris does not have formal training as a philosopher. Her comments about values such as honesty, integrity, or happiness do not appear in a theoretical framework. Yet, in her own way, she characterizes the dilemma we all have with ideals: holding to them as a matter of principle versus compromising them as a matter of practicality. She discussed how compromising our values can hurt us, but that hurt is sometimes valuable.

LVVL is a series intended for young readers of all ages looking for inspiration not only for course papers but also for their lives. The value of thoughtful reflection, not conversion, is the aim.

Richard Thompson Hull
Tallahassee, Florida

INTRODUCTION

As a young adult, I had a naive notion that chemistry would help solve some planetary problems, resulting in a better life for people. I became a chemist. Instead of being part of a solution, I became increasingly disturbed that my job as industrial chemist was contributing to the problem.

Then I thought I could do my part to help find some solutions by becoming a teacher in the local high school, but I was passed over for that job, I thought possibly because I was "overqualified." What I considered a curse at that time turned out to be one of the greatest blessings of my life.

So I decided to be a writer and wrote a book.

With the third rejection slip in hand, I began thinking again, "What now?" Having failed three times at what I thought I *really* wanted to do, what did I really *really* want to do?

Europe had always piqued my curiosity and I had great interest in the Holy Lands of Israel, Jordan, and Palestine. I checked my finances and figured I could travel for three or four months.

At first, my horizon was no farther than Europe and the Holy Land. I went down to New York City and found the *S.S. United States* was leaving in two days' time. I boldly bought the cheapest ticket and two days later sailed into what turned out to be my great adventure. To my delighted surprise, my three or four months' budget stretched to nearly a year.

I seized as many opportunities as possible to view the great "wonders" of the world. As I hiked and gazed at these wonders, I contemplated the philosophical and practical issues that had urged me on my pilgrimage.

When I started traveling in 1955, I was in anguish over what I viewed as severe and wide-ranging socioeconomic and political problems in the United States. I had a grandiose notion of returning from my travels with ideas about how to correct our faults as a nation. If I ever found a country that appeared to have avoided or eliminated these problems in its society, I even considered renouncing my American citizenship for that Shangri-la.

In addition, I yearned to retrace the roots of our political order. That meant starting with Great Britain. That initial visit suited my purposes well. I learned *so much*. The real revelation for me there was that while we in the United States are so conscious of our problems, Britain has problems as bad as ours, but the Britons did not appear to realize that they had problems at all. As for the French, the ones I talked to did recognize that they had problems, but had nothing I could see as a solution for ours. In the Netherlands, I viewed their dike system as a great achievement in social engineering. I admired the collective will required to accomplish the feat more than the technological achievement.. Everywhere I went, just an ordinary private person, I was always welcomed. Most often civil servants stopped working and talked on the spot. Some even escorted me, acting as guide sometimes.

I find that the usual obstacle to travel is that people think of "travel" as booking tours through an agency. Those trips include first-class accommodations and frills that I forewent on my journeys. By contrast, I often stayed in hostels; rarely ate in restaurants; rode third class, sometimes even in steerage; and sometimes hitchhiked to save money. In those days hitchhiking ("auto stopping") was a more accepted practice not as fraught with such dangerous risks as it is today. I did "splurge" in one way sometimes though: Some third-class "native" hotels that were as cheap as hostels had no single rooms, but placed three or four patrons in the same room. I drew the line at that, offering to pay for all the beds. The proprietor would usually promise not to rent the other beds but still refused the proffered extra money.

Even without being able to speak the language of the locales, to my knowledge, no one ever once cheated me. I found nearly everywhere people were great: kind, helpful, honest, and decent. I would hold out a handful of money, and they picked out some. I used "signs" to indicate my needs.

Of course, this crude method of communication precluded lofty discourses about ideas. Thankfully, many people I met around the world, especially at universities, were multilingual and spoke English as well as their native tongue. So not being fluent, I found that language was a barrier of sorts on many occasions, but I did not find it to be a major problem.

A rough count shows that I have visited about sixty-seven countries, the major exceptions being Red China, Australia, New Zealand, and Antarctica.

I feel compelled to issue an admonishment to the readers. People experiencing the same event can come away with very different perceptions of the same reality. Over time, memories of what those perceptions were also vary greatly from one person to the next and change over time within an individual. Someone else making the same trip right beside me might have had a very different perception; you might say even a different experience. Likewise, someone sharing those experiences might have strikingly different memories about the experiences years later. My memories have changed over time.

This is an account of my memories of how I perceived my travels as I remember them now. While I treasure honesty and accuracy, truth about the distant past is, by its nature, selective and subjective, and filtered by ensuing experience. Thus, I cannot be sure how well I succeeded at achieving accuracy.

Therefore, I warn the reader to take these memoirs with a grain of salt. If, as I would be, you are not satisfied with my account, I encourage you to go "see for yourself!"

One

POLICE ENCOUNTERS

Because I have always striven to be an extremely law-abiding person at home and abroad, any police encounter comes to me as a shock and then burns itself into my memory. In retrospect many years later, these memories remain so vivid that I have elected to recount them first. Although the memoirs overall are not presented in chronological order, these events, which occurred between 1955 and 1967, are presented in chronological order. Still, the specific dates are not as significant as the experiences. Those remain timeless in my mind.

These encounters took place both in the United States and abroad. The experiences were not all at the hands of police. Some were at the hands of other government officials who had authority to exercise power and control over me. In distant lands or close to home, confronted by police or by others in power positions, I perceived each of the experiences in much the same way.

Not so many years after I completed my graduate education I visited Puerto Rico as a sort of introduction to a locale with exotic tropical foreign flavor in a place that was still a part of the United States. While in Puerto Rico I decided to visit the Dominican Republic. From there I returned to mainland United States and was innocently walking along a sidewalk in a town north of Miami, Florida, on US Route 1—a route along which I traveled on my return to New York because of my love of historic or famous roads.

Suddenly a police car pulled over to me. Two police officers jumped out. They ordered me to get in the back seat of their car. Frightened, but knowing I had done nothing wrong, I obeyed their command. Suddenly I found myself for the first time in my life in a vehicle equipped with a security screen to prevent contact between the police and their prisoner and with doors that would not open from the inside—trapped!

Mystified, I sputtered questions about why I was being treated this way. Their only response was, "Where are your red shorts?" Their questioning confused me. Moreover, it got me raging at what I perceived to be a violation of my civil liberties—and I said so.

One of the officers said with a snarl, "One of *them*, eh?"

Meanwhile, the officers had checked my wallet and found only a small amount of U.S. currency—but enough to get me to New York—and a bit of Dominican currency. That seemed to arouse their suspicions, especially when I admitted that I had just returned from a visit there.

My fearful imagination wondered if they thought I was involved with some illegal drug trade.

Suddenly, the car screeched to a stop as the driver shouted, "There she is!"

In an instant, I realized what must be happening and why. A brunette woman we saw on the street was wearing red shorts with her hair coiffed in a coronet braid. There I sat, a brunette, wearing my hair in a coronet braid!

Greatly relieved, I saw at once that this must be a case of mistaken identity. The police appeared to realize their error at nearly the same moment. I think they considered letting me go at once, on the spot, but then decided to allow some higher authority to make that decision.

At the police station, the story of my Dominican Republic visit and my wallet containing foreign currency attracted some bit of attention, but shortly I was free to go.

Free! Mine was just a brief police encounter with an agreeably satisfying resolution—perhaps—but distinctly memorable because it was my first.

❦❧

The second encounter was much more serious and frightening to me. Occurring in Yugoslavia, a foreign setting far from home, served to intensify my fear.

In Trieste, Italy, on the frontier between Italy and Yugoslavia, I had cleared immigration and was looking for the currency exchange, which every frontier in Europe had right at the border for convenience—except here. No currency exchange bureau! What to do?

While I was puzzling over my dilemma, a voice speaking familiar American English hailed me. "Hi! American, aren't you?" My shoes and backpack must have been the giveaway. I nodded and explained my currency exchange problem. Cheerfully he said, "Worse than that none is open; there is no bus until tomorrow. But I can change some for you and give you a lift to Belgrade."

"Fine!" I replied, and hopped in.

Now my memory fails me about just what amount in American Express travelers checks I changed to dinars, but it was not much as I did not intend to stay long in Yugoslavia. I intended to move on by land to the Holy Land.

While later I wondered whether he was truthful, the stranger who offered me the ride told me that he was the third assistant secretary of the U.S. Embassy in Belgrade. To meet a personable young man in our diplomatic service was quite a heady experience for me at the time, and I took him at his word.

Some time around four in the morning, the man dropped me off at a hotel. As soon as he left, I intended to go the other way, to do something I longed to do even more than sleep: to see the sunrise over the Danube River.

I have always doted on rivers—and mountains and waterfalls, and historic sites. That dawn over the Danube was a thrilling adventure for me! Like a then-popular pop song said, I witnessed for myself that the Blue Danube is not blue but brown. I would have been content to linger longer, but hunger drove me to find some store with bread and cheese.

To my dismay, that day I discovered that cheese was not available, only butter. Normally I dislike butter on bread, but in unfamiliar lands, hunger confronted by limited availability dictates taste. Voila! I found it delicious!

How the butter was made in Yugoslavia for that day's feast I know not, but nowhere else in the world then or since have I found butter that I enjoyed as much. If the shopkeeper had not told me it was butter, I would have believed it to be some kind of cheese, rich and solid, not greasy. Later I did find cheese there. Through Greece and the Middle East, they enjoy what we Americans call goat feta cheese, but for the moment, I delighted that the butter was better than what I knew from home.

Before long, time pressed me to continue my journey for which I chose the fabled Orient Express to visit the Greek frontier.

Unfortunately, any resemblance between the luxurious image that the Orient Express may bring to mind and the hard seats in the third-class section at that time is purely coincidental. The actual physical discomfort of the seats was not as dismal as my shattered idealized mental image of the fabled locomotive.

My fellow passengers were, as usual, eager to practice their command of English conversation with personal questions such as, "Are you married?" "No." "How many children do you have?" "None." On this particular Yugoslav train ride, several people asked me about the annual production of sunflower seeds in America. I have no idea why sunflower seed production was so important them, but I suspect that many had studied from the same basic English conversation dialogues in their schoolbooks, learning to recite the most basic and sometimes odd questions that were standard in their texts.

The train made a stopover of an hour or two in the town of Skopje, Yugoslavia (now Macedonia). Needing to replenish my food supply, I stopped at the first shop to which I came, very near the station. Although unable to translate the words on the sign in the window, the number of dinars was, to my good fortune—or so I thought—in Arabic numerals. Doing a rough conversion of dinars to dollars, I calculated that a pound of salami from a deli in the United States would cost approximately the same number of dollars as a pound of salami in Yugoslavia cost in dinars. This surprised me because I had expected food in the Communist third world to be relatively cheap.

Resigned to the unexpectedly high cost, I put the correct number of dinars in my hand and pointed to the sign and then the meat in the case. The shopkeeper sliced off a large hunk of salami, then added more. Having no skill in the language, I had no way to tell her that she had already sliced off too much, and I worriedly expected a demand for additional dinars. To my surprise, she wrapped the package and accepted only the dinars in my hand.

Only as I left did I realize that the price, instead of being calculated per pound, was instead based on kilos; quite a bargain. Even as I marveled at the inexpensive prices, I wondered how I would ever eat that much salami! I also purchased a round loaf of bread, quite large, but they had no other. Satisfied that I had enough food for some time because salami keeps well—I used it often on backpacking trips—I returned to the station.

Back at the train station, I saw a peculiar kind of pump or faucet that produced a large flow of clear water for drinking. By this time, I needed a wash. I dug a washcloth and bar of soap out of my pack, washing there as thoroughly as I was able. Then I noticed beside me a man who looked as if he envied my soap, needing a wash himself. I offered the bar to him. He gratefully accepted, conveying wordlessly his smiling gratitude.

Suddenly there was a queue of people by us, each hoping to soap up with that one bar. Each would lather up, rinse, and then pass the soap to the person next in line. When finally the soap made its way back to me, it was no longer a bar but a tiny sliver. The workers' state paradise may have been good for providing bread and meat at affordable prices but appeared very lacking in soap.

Cleansed and satisfied from hunger sated, I was back on the train to continue my journey. Upon reaching the frontier checkpoint, two police officers motioned me with rifles to accompany them. I was bewildered. They indicated that I should bring my backpack with me. They took me to an interrogation room, allowing the train to continue without me, adding a sense of being stranded in a strange land to my growing sense of fear.

I became increasingly frightened as I sensed the situation to be quite serious. Their concern turned out to be a matter of currency control. They had counted my traveler's checks, found them discrepant, and I had no currency control document to account for the discrepancy, having made the private exchange with the young man whom I had met at the Trieste frontier.

Without warning my morals and my value system were challenged to an extent I would never have imagined possible. Crucial to my code of ethics, I never lie—never. Also having a sense of "my country, right or wrong," I wanted to protect the young man whom I believed worked for the U.S. Embassy.

The problem to my way of thinking was that since the young man was an official representative of the United States in Yugoslavia (even as I entertained this rationalization I began to question his credibility), I reasoned that would make any illegal money changing not his personal act, but an act of the United States. To my mind, I could not let the United States get in trouble on my account if I had any opportunity to avoid such trouble, even at great cost to my conscience and psyche.

Moreover, I passionately believed that if a person is judged wrongly, that person should struggle to right the wrong and bear the situation as best he or she can until the matter is resolved.

Feeling very virtuous and holding all those lofty values when they had never before been tested proved quite a different matter from clinging to them when alone, isolated, and stranded, confronted by intimidating police authorities in a foreign, especially communist, third world country.

Yes, take action to right the wrong, but what action? I envisioned that such a struggle might take years and in a flash, I saw that I had to act *now*. Given the alternatives, I broke my moral code and flat out lied—and would again if similar urgent circumstances appeared to impel it.

I expostulated that I just could not remember what happened to those missing traveler's checks. Throughout their intense questioning, I held to my story. Eventually they relented and when the next train came through, they marched me aboard. I was greatly relieved and perhaps they were too, to be rid of such a stubborn Yankee they felt convinced was lying.

In reviewing the incident later, I felt resentment because the complaint was not over some exorbitant sum such as the financiers who trafficked in millions of dollars or dinars. For my missing fifty dollars, I could not understand why all the fuss. The thought occurred to me that the police might have staged the entire scenario as a ruse to extort a bribe, that if I offered one, he might release me to catch the next train. Offering a bribe would also have gone against my moral code but not to the extent as the lying that hurt me so.

Incidentally, as near as I could tell, the young American in Trieste did not cheat me nor could have made anything on the black market from my travelers checks, though I did wonder where he changed my travelers checks or got a currency control document for them. One thing is certain. After that bitter experience, I never again exchanged currency illegally while abroad.

Back aboard, as I went in search of a comfortable compartment, I experienced a pleasant chance encounter that would never have occurred had the police not detained me. Scanning faces of likely seat companions, I saw a young Brit whom I thought I had met months before at Cambridge and so let out a delighted whoop, "Why, hello, X!"

Upon closer inspection, despite considerable resemblance, I saw that this man was not the same person whom I had met previously. I faltered, "Oh, I thought you were X that I met at Cambridge, but I see you're not." He replied, "Oh, you mean Lord Somename. Yes, lots of people mix us up because our mothers are identical twins. We look quite alike." "Lord Somename!" I exclaimed, "My goodness, he never let on he is a *peer*! I never met a British peer before!" "Impressed, eh?" he asked, somewhat amused. "You Yanks are so impressed by titles!"

What a great way to meet another personable young man, I thought, cousin to British nobility no less. The great beginning to a companionable group continued as the other occupants of the car were two Yugoslav men who had no English but another great gift: tomatoes, onions, cucumbers, and wine. For my contribution I still had my precious loaf of bread and plenty of salami. Being a teetotaler, I drank water from my canteen with purification tablets, foregoing the wine. We ate and partied until we fell asleep.

Lord Somename's cousin was heading for a religious retreat on Mount Athos, center of Eastern Orthodox Monasticism, located on the Athos peninsula of the larger Chalkidiki peninsula in the Macedonian region of Greece. My eventual destination was the Holy Land, traveling there in slow stages with many stops along the way. I had never thought of my trip as a religious retreat, but in chatting with my new friend I supposed it must have been. We disembarked from the train in Saloniki, Greece, and stayed a few days in a pension with which my new friend was familiar. It was very good and much cheaper than a hotel. When the desk clerk learned that I was going to Istanbul, Turkey, she gave me the address of a pension there. We spent our days walking and talking on a thin strip beach, resting with our backs against a wall to admire the sparkling light-blue Aegean with the sun glinting on the surface. The water was so light and bright I could not understand why Homer wrote of it as wine-dark. We only had a few days as we had to be on our way. For me, those few days had been a blissful interlude. My friend's train was going in one direction and mine in another. I would continue east to the *real* foreigners, the Turks of Istanbul.

As the train pulled out, my friend yelled out the window, "And I am Lord Anothername! So now you can really impress your Yankee friends with *two* British peers!" My last image of him was moving away from me, laughing. That British sense of humor—I *love* it! To this day, I do not know why it never once occurred to me during our time together that he might also have been a peer. I was glad not to have known sooner. To me he was just my friend. Knowing before our respite might have changed the experience.

❧❦

Leaving Yugoslavia behind did not spell the end of confrontational police encounters for me. That 1956 trip was just before the Suez War of Israel. After leaving Saloniki, I was on the main road frontier of Turkey on my way to cross into Syria.

In all other crossings, except that terrifying Yugoslav one, customs may have asked me to open my pack, but that was about it. Here, though, Turkish customs officials took out each item and shook it. I supposed this was a drug search but on leaving instead of entering? I felt okay with the process until they got to my Bible and my underwear.

The majority of Turks were then Muslim, but the country was secular. I fathomed no way that my personal religious material, as opposed to a large number for distribution, could matter, could it? Still they waved my Bible around and made jeering remarks. They appeared to be replaying ancient Turkish-Christian animosity that I had supposed went out with Mustafa Kemal Atatürk.

How they handled my undergarments really incensed me. They made pretense of putting it on and danced around! Never anywhere else in the whole world has anything like that happened to me, before or since. Still, that was not yet the worst blow.

I had no exit visa. No one had ever mentioned that I needed one. I could not leave Turkey until I obtained one. Imprisoned in a whole country? How could they do that? I quickly learned that countries can do nearly anything they wish with their own people or helpless foreigners in their midst.

No other option was open to me than to return all the way to Ankara, Turkey, to obtain an exit visa. That was a long distance, causing considerable delay.

Coming back, I did not want to pass through the same customs post to face their insults again. Instead, I changed my route over to a small Turkish frontier town, with a lesser road into Syria. There I found to my dismay a sign: "Frontier closed." I asked, "When will it open?" With a shrug, "Maybe tomorrow"—or the next day, or the next.

My options limited to one, I hiked back the mile or so into Gevgeli, found a hotel room, and waited. Actually, I enjoyed the three days that I was there. There was a balcony outside the room from which I could look down at the people in the street—fascinating parade. Moving a little table out to the balcony, I could write about whatever sparked my fancy.

Each morning I hiked to the frontier to be greeted with the shrugged "Maybe tomorrow." I was at the point of swallowing my rage to return to the more used post (now that I had the document to shove in their faces) when finally I heard, "Yes, open, you can cross." I steeled myself for the reexamination of my pack, but they barely opened it, and I was on the shuttle bus for the three miles of no-man's land between the Turkish and Syrian frontier posts.

The frontier post fences were covered with barbed wire. I shuddered. Land mines out there, too? I knew that Turkey was "surrounded by enemies." That was not mere paranoia. Neither Turks nor Arabs easily forgot the enmity stirred up by Lawrence of Arabia's breakup of the sultan's Turkish empire or Turkey as a German ally being conquered in that war. There may have been more recent enmity between Turkey and Syria, too, but I was not that well informed on the (eternal?) enmities of Middle Eastern nations, of which Turkey, I think, would like to consider itself not one of "them." Still, I had never seen such a demarcation between countries, nor have I since.

I passed through the Syrian frontier post without incident and heaved a sigh of relief as I headed to the bus for Aleppo, Syria, from where I could go on to Damascus or the rest of Syria. I relaxed too soon for the worst was yet to come.

As I was about to get on the bus, a man in blue suit came to me with my name and a question mark in his voice, although he was obviously certain of my identity. I wondered, "Now how in the world?" but he had me penned there and I was obviously the only foreigner. Mystified, I assented. He whipped out a paper in Arabic, which meant nothing to me except for three words in roman there in its middle: my name.

To say alarm shot through me is a gross understatement. As he moved to get the document, his jacket opened slightly, allowing me to glimpse a shoulder holster with pistol. I gulped. Guns do that to me. What I could not decide was whether the glimpse had been accidental or if he had deliberately planned for me to see the gun as a show of force.

Another thing guns do to me is make me an arrant coward. The man motioned me into the bus to a window seat, while he took the aisle seat. Since the bus was going to Aleppo, I supposed for some reason I could not fathom he was taking me to a police station there. I had heard of Communist activity in Syria, but I could not complete any coherent thought. One of the frontier post soldiers with a rifle whom I had seen was accompanying us. I realized that this was a genuine police encounter of a most serious kind!

I had not the slightest inkling of what the trouble could possibly be. From that first aborted attempt to get from Turkey to Syria through the three days waiting in Gevgeli to cross into Syria, there had been ample time for my name to have come up somehow—but why on earth should it have? I brooded about making an escape to go to the U.S. consul in Aleppo or the Ambassador in Damascus, but my escorts had the pistol and rifle.

By the time we came to Aleppo, darkness had fallen. I supposed the man would herd me to the police station but to my shock we went to a hotel instead. Maybe they meant to put me up till morning under guard. So I was not too surprised to be herded into a room there. But this room had three beds. That did surprise me some. Then I was utterly shocked when they began to take off their clothes to change into pajamas, indicating for me to do likewise.

Rest assured they appeared not to have anything like sex in mind, and oddly enough, I did not even think that they might. Fortunately I had slept in trail shelters with men and women in sleeping bag proximity enough that mixed-gender close quarters never bothered me. What did bother me was the pistol and rifle. Since our backs were turned from each other, I did not see whether my guard kept on his shoulder harness and holster for the pistol. My last waking thought was the silly thought that if he did, it must be so uncomfortable!

The next morning, I opened my eyes to solitude. The other two beds were empty. Pistol, rifle, men, and their little bags were gone. What on earth was going on? I did not waste a minute to think but shoved clothes into the pack and hurried out and down the stairs to the street, heading to a bus for Damascus. I made it without further incident.

To this day I have no clue as to what this Syrian encounter meant. I toyed with the thought that Syria had something like a tourist bureau and was trying to attract tourists by showing us how the country was safe for travel, but that seemed ridiculous: be kind to tourists with guns? Rather long later, I thought maybe it was Arab-Syrian hostility to Jews, and they thought I might be a Jewish spy with that Bible as cover, but then decided that explanation made no sense either.

Hostility seems eternally endemic to the Middle East, and this was an especially hostile time, though I did not know that then. The 1956 war, not to be confused with the Six-Day War in 1967, from which Israel gained the Old City and other territory, broke out just a few weeks later. Whatever the reason, the Syrian encounter remains to this day a complete mystery to me.

🐾

It must have been the exotic frontier character that attracted me to live in Alaska for three years between 1957 and 1960 despite my usual claim that I never do anything for adventure. There were certainly other aspects, such as a genuine desire to do my part to ameliorate injustices suffered by the people already in Alaska when the first European settlers arrived on the American East Coast, not many years before Russian fur traders were despoiling Alaska's West Coast. Anyway, I was living in a compound that had been a naval installation but turned, after World War II, into a boarding high school for Alaskan natives where I taught.

The school had a two-week summer vacation during which most of the teachers flew to visit to relatives. I chose instead to see something of the vast territory for it would be such a shame to return for good to the lower forty-eight only to confess that I had not seen a thing of Alaska except that tiny compound. So I traveled around Alaska and on the way back to work took the Alcan Highway from Fairbanks, Alaska, to the Yukon border, intending from there to make my way farther along the same route into the Yukon to a cross-road, the Haines Cutoff, and then back into Alaska at the town called Haines at the head of the fjord called Lynn Canal.

This was the take-off point to go over White Pass into Dawson City, Alaska, of gold-rush days. I would have loved to continue from the Alaskan border on the Alcan to Dawson and then through this pass into Haines, but time was pressing. Although now there is a tourist train, there was not then, so I do not know how I would have accomplished that entire trip in one two-week jaunt.

As with many Americans, before I went to Alaska, the vastness of the distances and the sparseness of the population along the Canadian and Alaskan borders up there just did not sink in. At that time, after the train to Fairbanks, no public transportation was available between there and—I do not know where in Canada. So how did I manage?

Carriers took mail along the Alcan Highway from Fairbanks to the roadhouse on the Yukon border at Scotty Creek one day and back the next day after overnight there—but never on Sundays. The highway was a gravel road with periodic "roadhouses" that served as gasoline and service station, trading post, motel, and camping facilities. These were necessary for travelers in case of car trouble along the highway. Except for them and some remote trappers' cabins, there was nothing but forest for nearly five hundred miles.

The mail route was a star route, which meant by contract. The carrier could carry passengers for a fee as well as mail. I rode with the U.S. mail as far as the border. (In the United States, Canada, and Mexico we speak of "borders"; throughout the rest of the world, they speak of "frontiers.")

Upon reaching the border roadhouse, I was in luck for there was a charter tour bus going to Dawson the next day. The driver allowed me to ride (on the back seat so not to interfere with the tourists) as far as the Haines Cutoff, where I assumed there would be another roadhouse in case I did not catch a lift into Haines. Traversing approximately two hundred miles, I saw only three or four cabins along the way.

This road and the Alcan on the Canadian side were both open to the public only in summer. In winter the road was open for mail delivery on the Alaskan, but not the Canadian side. I deduced the United States was more concerned to get mail to its citizens in remote Alaska than the much-touted British-Canadian Her Majesty's Mail Service worried about getting mail to her Yukon Territory citizens in winter.

I found no roadhouse at that location. I was alone in a *vast* wilderness. True, there would be no darkness to add to the anxiety, I had emergency food, and a canteen of water, and I had been assured that animals about were safe at that time of year. Still, I confess to feeling anxious as the tour bus pulled away.

Luckily, I had nearly no time to be afraid because as I contemplated my fate a dirty rattletrap white Ford came up on the other side of the road and made a U-turn over to me. Signage on the Ford read "Royal Canadian Mounted Police." He was, oh, perhaps fiftyish and fat, with a great paunch hanging over his belt of a sort of ragtag brownish (and dirty?) uniform jacket and trousers, and—did he have on sneakers or just street shoes?—with all this, he was smoking a big, fat, foul cigar.

This was quite a contrast to my mental image of a slim, handsome Nelson Eddy-type young man donned in scarlet coat, blue breeches, and shiny black boots mounted on a handsome horse and beautiful Collie waiting to be a hero, with a beautiful woman in the background, and then the Mountie gets the prize while singing beautiful duets. So much for images.

Predictably, the Mountie wanted to know what I was doing out there in this vast wilderness alone. No doubt he sensed a duty to me if I were stranded somehow and needed help. The nearest roadhouse was a far distance away by foot.

I explained my optimistic plan. The Mountie agreed that chances were fair that there would be a vehicle going down to Haines sometime and would surely pick me up. Even those afraid of hitchers would surely not speed by a lone woman in such a wilderness.

Thus, in a few minutes my Royal Canadian Mounted Police encounter ended without incident. Sure enough, shortly after, I did get that lift to Haines.

This was not a terrifying or dangerous encounter as some of the others in my life had been. How I thought about this brief encounter changed after experiencing its sequel.

Back in the schoolroom, I told the students about my meeting with the Mounted Police while I stood alone in the wilderness. On of my students said, "Aw, Ms. Harris, he thought you were one of us at first!"

Revelation. Along with many fair-skinned American ancestors, I have a native ancestor whom I tend to favor much more than the blonde side of the family. I do not think it is that little touch of oppressed minority in me that makes me so concerned to rectify wrongs done to minorities as much as I can, but the student's comment made me wonder whether the Mountie had stopped me at first because he was suspicious of natives.

Indeed, recently the problem of "racial profiling" has come to national attention. This was what my young student meant.

That border is totally without delineation, except at that one point on the Alcan Highway. Canadian and Native American people cross at will. On the Alaskan side, one U.S. Marshal covered a territory of a thousand square miles. Border enforcement could not be strict. U.S. Coast Guard along or in coastal towns probably react the same way. In the Eastern United States, this practice suffered by African-Americans and Hispanics. In western states and Alaska, it would be brown-skinned native peoples more often the victims of police encounters. How sad.

☙━❦

The Syrian encounter should have prepared me for the Jordanian police encounter, but did not. Despite my previous encounters, I was complacent and felt safe. After all, I was there for the same reason that Christian pilgrims have gone since Helena, mother Constantine the Great, made her pilgrimage in the fourth century CE. Surely others completed the pilgrimage before then, and there has been steady stream since.

On the bus from Amman, Jordan, to Jericho, Palestine, we had a passport control check at a humdrum bridge across a little muddy stream. It was not until the bus was going on that I "woke up" in shock and turned back for a fast look at the quickly disappearing view. The Jericho bus stop being still a mile distant, we had just crossed the Allenby Bridge over the River Jordan, a famous dream river to the Promised Land for nearly three millennia and I had nearly missed the sight!

At that time Jericho and the Mount of Temptation were in the state of Jordan. In Jericho I was thrilled to spy a large tree behind a wall of a courtyard with big, easily climbable branches overhanging the street. "Zaccheus' tree!" I thought. Obviously it could not literally been the same tree of the Bible story, but that did not matter to me. I could imagine Zaccheus, the tax collector, up on a big branch of that tree, hoping to catch a glimpse of Jesus as he passed and his life-changing encounter with the Lord—not with any police, Jordanian or otherwise.

Seeing that tree alone made my entire trip to the Holy Land worthwhile.

While in Jordan, I visited one of the sites of the baptism and even swam across the River Jordan. As I experienced the baptismal sites in Jordan, and even later at several similar sites in Israel, I marveled that such a comparatively small river could loom so large in importance. There is no accounting for religious sensibilities and the hold that religion holds over human emotions. For the record, the Jordan is not only religiously significant but important for irrigation, so much so that Israel and the Arab countries have to have United Nations' supervision of water withdrawal.

Another big attraction near Jericho is Mount Quarantania, believed by some to be the site of the Temptation of Christ. Naturally I had to make the climb, not arduous. There are many paths up, down, and across. I camped out at the summit for a few nights, very pleasurably except for my meditation on the Temptation and sin. In the hot desert terrain I found there I could always find a boulder that provided shade in which to rest and usually a faint breeze. I worried that water might be a problem, but it was not. A few minutes' walk down was Elisha's Fountain, another biblical site not well known at that time, with cool, sweet water. The fountain is in a grove of fig trees.

Like Nathaniel, I sat under a fig tree, gazing up at the Mount. I mused that perhaps I sat under the same tree as Nathaniel did—who could prove otherwise? I found the grove to be the very best place to be on a hot, hot day!

Securing food in Jericho was easy. First, I hiked into Jericho to buy bread and cheese. In addition, both under the fig tree and especially atop the Mount in the shade of a boulder, there were numerous people passing to and fro to get water from the fountain and rest a while. At the top, many young boys where herding goats. In the tradition of true Arab hospitality, several offered me food that they all appeared to carry.

I concluded this particular mountain could hardly be the site of the Temptation of Christ, including near starvation, unless he just refused offers of food sharing. The place is very near the civilization of Elisha's Fountain and Jericho and has been since the time of Joshua. Seeing the reality almost demands that that the Bible story be read metaphorically, which is fine with me. I read it that way before being there, but more especially since.

Camping out on Mount of Temptation and passing time under a fig tree at Elisha's Fountain was an idyllic interlude. While I was there, a handsome young Jordanian who spoke excellent English came by, a good prospect with whom to pass the time of day. Instead of continuing my camping, he invited me to be a guest in his home. I declined, saying that I would never accept such an offer without an invitation from his mother. He told me that his mother was dead, but he appreciated the stipulation and remarked that my refusal evinced a good moral code, one he claimed to share.

The man lived with his sister, a nurse at the local hospital: Surely she would be a permissible chaperone? He left to bring his sister back for the invitation. This time I accepted. Thus I enjoyed a few days and nights as a guest in the home of these two Jordanians. When they went to work, I spent my time in the fig grove, returning to their home in the evenings. My desire was not to seek out a free hotel. I offered, as was my habit, to pay for my expenses, but they graciously declined my offer. I relished the opportunity to live with Arabs in their home instead of only meeting them while passing through the area as a member of a tour group.

So you ask me, how did the police come into this idyllic picture? One evening, perhaps the second evening of my stay, a knock came at the door. The man and his sister exchanged the question, "Who can that be?" only to find the police at the door.

The police demanded to see my passport and after inspecting it, confiscated it from me. I was appalled! I think they said I could get it back when I was ready to leave the country. In the meantime, however, I was unable to stay to travel to other sites in Jordan because just about anywhere might have passport control.

Although I had not especially wanted to see most of those sites because they were not biblically connected, I had wanted to visit the biblical town of Jarash, Jordan (formerly Gerasa, Syria), in the area once known as the Decapolis, the name given in the Bible and by ancient writers to a region in Palestine lying to the east and south of the Sea of Galilee. Some ruins there lie in a remote, quiet valley among the mountains of Gilead. Having my passport confiscated made me feel quite deprived of my autonomy.

I decided that I would go the next day to the authorities to plead my case. I planned to tell them that I did not wish to leave Jordan yet, but that I wished to leave Jericho for Jerusalem's Old City, a most significant destination for me; therefore, could I please have the passport?

I did not have the chance to carry out my plan because early the next morning the police returned. This time they indicated for me to leave with them and to bring my pack. My hosts and I were quite glum about my being carried away by the police. I was powerless to act in any way but had to obey.

To my dismay, the police put me in a cell of the Jericho jail. The cell had a cot, one straight chair, and pot in the corner. I do not recall water arrangements for drinking and washing. Eventually I was brought a plate of food—an excellent omelet with bread and tea. In a while someone came and took the empty plate away and I was left again, but not for long.

Soon they took me to an interrogation room and my tribulation began, not with any torture, just questions repeated over and over, and mostly the same question: "Why are you in Jordan?" I was so naive that I assumed tourists were pilgrims with only one reason to go there and to Israel: to walk where Jesus walked.

Sadly, the way the two countries had carved up the geo-political landscape, there was no way to take a biblical harmony and walk it in anything like chronological order, as, for example, from the reputed site of the Annunciation to the site of the Nativity, with a side trip to Egypt and then back to Nazareth, Israel, stopping at the sites of the Visitation and Presentation, not to mention retracing Jesus' travels around the Sea of Galilee. I asked, "Why else would anyone want to go there?"

The police did not seem satisfied with my answers. The interrogation dragged on and on, but finally they put me back into the cell. I began to experience the intense, horrifying terror that I might be in a Jordanian jail for a long time—and they never even offered to let me contact the American consul or ambassador. By international law they had to, didn't they?

I never saw a gun there, but I believed that even without my seeing any guns they certainly had them. With or without seeing weapons, I repeated my conviction that countries can do as they please with their own people or foreigners. I even felt worry about the blameless man and woman who were simply being hospitable to me. Might there be some nasty fallout onto them?

My anxiety and fear may have exaggerated my perception of how long I spent in the cell. The next time they came, they herded me out to a waiting car. At the door of the jail I saw my host. Perhaps he had come concerned about my welfare and was denied permission to talk with me. We quickly waved to each other as I was put into the car, to be driven where I had no idea.

Shortly I noticed that we were not going back to the river and Amman but forward, evidently to Jerusalem. Sure enough, soon I was hauled out at the American consulate there in the Old City. I had to wait in an anteroom for a brief time. The Jordanian official came back out from an office, never glancing my way as he passed me, and I was called into the office.

It is odd that I felt such strong negative emotion when a Jordanian official asked me questions. I thought of that as interrogation. When this American official asked me similar questions, I merely felt he was trying to get my side of the story, as indeed he was. But I could not pay full attention to his words because there on his desk I spied my passport.

After the official expressed sympathy that, of course, Americans or any others have a right to tour the land and sites they deem holy, he castigated me for having let the passport get out of my hands. In my mind I shouted, "But how in the world could I have stopped them from taking it? The officials have the right to see it—in their hands—and then if they keep it, I can hardly fight them to get it back!"

Aloud I meekly said, "But these were police and I always cooperate with police." Then he exploded, "Do not be too cooperative! Even with police outside the United States!" He sounded as if he were implying that police might be even worse than ordinary citizens by virtue of their power positions. I have since found out that yes, they can be. He continued that the passport did not belong to me but to the United States and I, or anyone entrusted with one, had the distinct and solemn duty to protect it—which I am very willing to do but still do not see how I could have wrested it back when the man held it. Of course, I did ask for it, but that consul seemed to imply, "Do not ask, scream. Threaten with the U.S. Army or the like."

That was the end of the consul's scolding. As he handed back the precious small booklet, he asked about details of my trip: Did I have a reservation somewhere here in the Old City? When I answered no, he sent me in a staff car to an Anglican pilgrimage hostel—very nice—just in time for supper there.

My first priority next morning was to hunt up a cheaper pension off an alleyway there in the Old City, at which I stayed between trips to the "traditional" sites in the rest of then Jordan until I was reluctantly ready to go through Mandelbaum Gate into Israel, never to return I supposed. Years later, I did return when that gate had been torn down and Old City was in Israel.

Like the other encounters, I never forgot my Jordanian police encounter; the memories remain vivid.

∽⁓

The next "police" encounter was the most frightening yet, the one I call the "Moscow Incident," but I never found out whether it was a police encounter at all.

In 1960, I spent two months in the Soviet Union to study their culture and form of government. I took some courses, including Russian, in which I became proficient enough to read *Pravda* but never to use effectively. I discovered a few years later that the literacy I had achieved then had lapsed into total illiteracy.

At that time, Intourist USSR, a Florida-based travel operator, arranged all foreigners' travel in the then Soviet Union, first class, of course. I booked a trip, but this meant that I was constrained to limit my exploration to the pace of the group. It was frustrating to me, as the guide was always late. Inwardly I fumed at the thought of wasting time better spent learning new things.

Occasionally I took the opportunity to escape the Intourist officiousness, but not often. I knew that the intention was not to check up on us but to be helpful. No foreigner ignorant of Russian could successfully navigate travel in the Soviet Union without a fluent guide to replace our use of aids we ordinarily take for granted, such as the ability to find an address using a telephone book.

In 1922, the Soviet Union had established the Young Pioneers as a mass youth organization for children between the ages of ten and fifteen, where they inculcated children with generally wholesome citizenship values along with Soviet Communism doctrine. The government built many Pioneer Palaces, centers for extramural education and activities, with sections for creative work and sports. While children who excelled in academic study, work, sports, or social activity were rewarded, the primary purpose of the organization was to prepare children for entrance into the Komsomol, the youth arm of the Communist Party.

I had heard of the Soviet Young Pioneers as comparable to our Boy and Girl Scouts and had wanted to visit a Pioneer Palace. For no given reason, our guide kept putting me off. So I went on my own—no trouble at all to find one—and I went in with no one ever paying the slightest attention to me. I think the employees supposed I was some inspector from their administrative ministry. From what I had heard, I gathered that perhaps they thought it best not to beg trouble by asking questions. Of course, the children would not notice just another adult around.

The palace was just a gymnasium with boys playing some ball game and other rooms much like classrooms where girls were doing embroidery or similar activities. This place did not appear to be like the Boy or Girl Scouts to me. The activities appeared comparable, in an opposite sort of way, to those of the children whom I had observed at play in Great Britain. There the girls were also active in sports, never at stitching (that I saw), and the locus of activity was usually unstructured, unsupervised, and out of doors. The Pioneer Palace that I visited had no grounds around it for any outdoor games.

The indoor-outdoor difference aroused my curiosity. Perhaps the difference paralleled the difference in climate, with Moscow winters so long and cold and British ones shorter and milder. Along that line I noticed another cultural difference. The Brits considered some cold a good thing to toughen themselves, while the Russians stayed close to their fires in over-heated rooms, avoiding cold as much as possible. This was my naive observation.

I should say that Intourist never flat out refused a request if the tourist was bold enough to voice one, although it was not uncommon for Intourist to merely put off the request indefinitely.

Thus I repeatedly asked for a train ticket on the Trans-Siberian Railroad, if only as far as Vladivostok, Russia, from which I could surely get some ship over to Japan, I supposed, or as far as they would let me go.

As I said, it was never a flat refusal. Instead, I would always hear some excuse like, "The agent is out now and won't be back until next Tuesday." On Tuesday, I would hear some other excuse. I finally gave up that train ride as wasting too much of my limited time and chose instead to go to Leningrad, Russia (now again St. Petersburg) to tour the Hermitage and other points of interest. I do not know how many trains ran between there and Moscow at the time, and I do not recall the ride from Moscow up. For the return trip, Intourist had booked me on a night train. Intourist never asked for preferences but acted as if they knew what was "best" for the tourist and supplied it. Therefore, I missed seeing the countryside, which I would have preferred.

This night train had an advantage that the day train might not have had. I was in a compartment with three young Russian men who spoke quite fluent English. Besides them there was a constant stream into our compartment—all night long!—of others eager to converse unrestrainedly with a Yankee.

I was in my usual questioning mode of trying to learn from them what they believed were the good features of Communism. They had a lot of talk but never came up with anything that impressed me much.

It intrigued me that they did not ask me in return what I found commendable about the United States. I supposed that they assumed any American would be so brainwashed that no answer would be worthwhile.

These intelligent, educated citizens of the Communist regime did not appear to simply parrot the party line. But here and everywhere else on that 1960 trip to the Soviet Union, I never once caught any hint of desire to change the system, only to improve it here and there. As I believed about my own so-called democratic system of government, so I supposed Communism was on the planet to stay for centuries to come. Thus, I was as shocked as the rest of the world when just thirty short years later came the fall of the Soviet Empire. As I write now, I wonder how the United States' "empire" will fare in this new millennium.

All this is a prelude to the terrifying Moscow incident, for the train arrived in Moscow just at dawn that day. The station was already crowded.

I had planned, now being out of Intourist clutches after they put me on this train to Moscow, to make my way to the other railroad station for a train to the Afghan frontier to continue overland through the famous Khyber Pass to India, on to Japan, and then home, all in slow stages. I would travel third class for both for the economy and to interact with the common people.

Immediately upon disembarking, my grand plan was shattered at once by someone calling my name, in English, and holding up a sign that had my name. My mind flooded with paranoid hypotheticals. Was this man of the KGB secret police? Having been scrupulously law-abiding in my past meant nothing; people can be framed by false evidence so easily. But why?

My irrational non-thinking began moving faster than the speed of light, fueled by memories of an American spy plane that had recently been shot down over Siberia. Instead of taking the cyanide capsule, the pilot, Gary Francis Powers, was captured and incarcerated in a Soviet prison.

Might the Soviet government want another incident, even if manufactured? I reacted purely instinctively or reflexively. Much quicker than this telling of the incident, I opened my mouth in a loud scream pointing to the man as though he had pinched me.

In a split second and without moral weighing, I had committed my second lie in a police encounter, by body language and scream, if not words.

The man blushed scarlet as the crowd turned to him while I made tracks away. I race-walked to avoid running, which might attract attention. I knew just where I was hurrying to, for this station was connected by tunnels both to the Moscow subway and to the Intourist hotel next to it, where I had stayed a week or so before.

These Intourist hotels had checkrooms where I checked my American suitcase to rid myself of my dead giveaway. To check in, I used the room number from my previous room, praying its present occupant would not also want to check a parcel and find this strange one bag already there.

As I gathered my wits, it came to me that probably the man was not KGB per se but an Intourist guide sent to "help" the foreigner he presumed otherwise helpless to get around. The assumption that I need help without my asking for it always did and still does infuriate me.

I thought that I might merely need to avoid the Intourist Guide and not escape the KGB. But at the time I was also keenly aware of a common notion that Intourist was a covert arm of the KGB—all the same.

It was to check out such common notions for myself that I went to the Soviet Union in the first place. Many years later, I realized, especially at its fall, that I had not really learned much at all, though at the time it seemed I was learning so much I could not take it all in.

While all these thoughts crowded my mind, I had also been thinking: Where can you hide in Moscow from the KGB? American Embassy? Not a hideout really, but a retreat. But my going there would require explaining.

Then the British Embassy just to hang out? No—too allied.

Aha! A neutral embassy!

India was, to my mind, a neutral country par excellence and I did intend to visit there, eventually. I decided this was an opportune time to visit to the Indian Embassy to get my visa and information.

After checking my bag, I hurried to the subway headed for the Indian Embassy. But how would I know how to get there or to find it without leaving a trail either the KGB or Intourist could follow?

I do not recall how I got to the Indian Embassy, before it opened, of course. That was fine with me, as I wanted breakfast, not in an Intourist hotel designed for us wealthy foreigners, but at a common restaurant where the people of the locale typically ate. Finding just such a place was no problem, and if anyone noticed my shoes that marked me as a foreigner, it did not come up. I dined there for breakfast and ordered some food to take out for my lunch since I wanted to avoid being on the streets until it was time to return to the train station.

My new itinerary included taking the Tashkent Express. From there I supposed I could take a local to the Afghan frontier. Having made a mental conversion from tourist to commuter, however, left me with no idea of the train schedule. Once in the station I did as many people did, camp and wait, mingling among the locals, trying to hide my shoes that were such a giveaway.

I believed that the Politburo put its money into the military and space programs and neglected decent shoes for the people. But many years later, in

2002, I met three young Russian women on educational visas here in the United States and their shoes were still, ah, peculiar. Perhaps the Russians just do not like substantial shoes like American and western Europeans wear when not dressing "fancy." But I digress.

At that time, Intourist required the tourist to pay in advance for hotels and meals for which they issued coupons. I used rubles for the workers' restaurant. While waiting for the train, I found an Intourist hotel far from both stations and the embassy where I ate and tried to get food to go. I was disappointed to learn that they had only bread and cheese, and no "take-out."

I still had some coupons left but decided if I could not use them I might have to let them go because I was going to use rubles for the train ticket. Using the coupons might leave an unwanted trail and I still sought to be cautious just in case Intourist officials were looking for me.

Returning to pick up my suitcase, I found to my relief that no one had questioned it. Quickly I went to the other railroad station.

Over the years, sometimes people have curiously asked me, "How could you get around like that?" Really, I do not know. I have always been able to get around any city without any trouble, with the exception of Hanoi and Ho Chi Minh City in Viet Nam, and Athens, Greece. I think the difference is that when I go on my own from, say, a railroad station to some address, I somehow get some sort of orientation to the map of it. But in the three cities I mentioned, I did not go on my own. Seeing sights only in a tourist bus, I never got that sort of orientation.

Regardless, I studied the boards and was in luck. The Tashkent left around midnight and the board gave me the price in rubles: I could get that and not have to call attention to my foreignness by open mouth. So I worked out the rubles for no change necessary and just waited until they called the train.

My plan worked out splendidly. I thought on the train that I was safe from pursuit if indeed there ever had been any. My brain told me and tells me now there was never any danger, but I was anxious anyhow.

That hard-seat train ride was one of my most memorable events in the Soviet Union. The people were very decent and friendly to me, as indeed I have found all over the world, except in Latin America, where I found strong anti-American sentiment, although I have heard that is changing—I hope.

Thus, this "police encounter" might have been merely my mistaken notion about the attempt to "help" me by an officious Intourist guide. I was terrified all the same. To this day, I still shiver at the memory.

It was in Myanmar at a small port town called Mergui that I had the *longest* police encounter: a whole week of what I call "house arrest." I never did know why. This was 1961. I was still on my way overland from Russia to

Hong Kong, Japan, and home. I had been enjoying a leisurely trip through Myanmar while making my way slowly south toward Malaysia, through which I intended to traverse on my way to Thailand if some bus crossing over the mountains into Thailand did not come first.

With this plan in mind, I had already traveled down the Irrawaddy River from Moulmein, Myanmar, and then took a train from Yongon, Myanmar; I guess it must have been to its southernmost railhead. My *National Geographic* map showed no road beyond, but I reasoned there had to be something: People seem to have a built-in compulsion to move from place to place. The map was just too small to show more. I was right. From that place people took to boats on a fluvial network south; as did I. How *delightful*!—and the price was low.

After a few days travel with natives on a small river boat, we finally came to the end of that segment of river travel at Mergui.

At Mergui I smelled trouble. I was right.

There was an official in a smart-looking uniform, obviously a military officer. With him was another soldier, carrying a rifle, in a grubby uniform, obviously an enlisted man. The officer spoke quite good English—and as in other places, he had my name and an order: He would drive me to the airport to fly back to Yongon.

Maybe I am just an arrogant, ugly American not used to being told what to do in that demanding way. I did not want to fly back to Yongon and said so, strongly. I asserted that I wanted to go either south into Malaysia or east into Thailand, that there *must* be some kind of transport, and if he would kindly find such transport for me I would take it at once and be away from there.

Oh, I should say that at the first he had demanded to see my passport and he kept it in his possession. Despite my bad experience in Jordan, I still naively expected him to hand it back to me while he explained there was no transport either east or south from Mergui. Without my passport, the only thing I could do was, as he had said, return to Yongon.

I think that is when I said, "And if I won't go?" He answered, "Then we hold you!" He did not use the word "arrest." That was when I asked how he could do that when I had broken no law. I was still convinced there *must* be transport to some place other than Yongon, as I had found that fluvial transport to this place merely by following people who seemed to know where they were going.

In response he simply held up my passport—quite like the Jordanian police—knowing I would be "held," as he said, without it. Then the officer motioned for the soldier with the rifle to take me—to his house!

Upon arrival I saw that the soldier had a wife and child about two years of age. He motioned me to a structure in the courtyard much like the fluvial network shelters, but it had a table, chair, water barrel, and screened corner. He left me there.

Shortly the wife came with the afternoon rice. To reach this shelter I had to climb some stairs. The higher elevation was designed evidently to catch the breeze. As jails go, this one was very comfortable. I just wondered which of us would cave in first about that passport. How many days could I afford to stay in this comfortable shelter-jail?

I vividly recalled the dressing down of that Jerusalem consul never to let the passport get out of my hands again, even (especially?) to the police of a foreign country. But how could I help it? Easy. Capitulate: Fly back to Yongon.

If the officer had offered the option of retracing my route on the fluvial network back to the railhead and then to Yongon by train, I might have capitulated just as I had retraced my route from the Afghan frontier back to Tashkent and then from the Syrian border back to Ankara for exit visas.

A crucial difference in my mind was that in the USSR at the Afghan frontier, they just told me I had to do it, leaving the means to me. In this case, the officer not only ordered me to go but he gave me no choice in how I would go. I balked against his arbitrary seizure of my autonomy.

That my situation constituted house arrest was definitely impressed on me the next morning as I casually attempted to leave through the gate just to see the port, for no way could I get far without my passport. But the soldier barred my way with his rifle. The next morning, I tried again and this time he let me go. I assumed he had consulted with the officer who advised him that I could not go far without my passport. From then I varied between scribbling at the table in my pleasant jail or going down to watch the scene of the little port and listening to the music of the pagoda bells.

But how long could this almost–Shangri-la house arrest possibly last before I caved in? Without my passport, I was helpless.

Meanwhile, knowing Myanmar to be one leg of the golden triangle of drug traffic, I was also conscience stricken. They could be making multiple copies of my passport for use by drug couriers. That might be what the Jerusalem consul had in mind, although he never mentioned it. I rationalized that it was no use to give in now, for any such damage would have already been done.

About a week later, the officer returned and I knew it was showdown time. The officer and the soldier herded me to the port and up the gangplank of a ship of the P&O Cruise Line heading south to the last stop in Myanmar and finally on to Australia. While still in Myanmar, but on the border with Malaysia, I could catch a bus to the border and another on the other side to Bangkok, Thailand.

I wanted to go deck passage with the Asians, but the officer said no, I must go first class with the Europeans. I had to accede to that and watched them take out the travelers checks to pay for my passage. The remainder they returned intact to me. (At this point so far removed in time from that day I do not recall that he had taken my traveler's checks, but the memory of his tearing out the checks for me to sign at the ship is still a very vivid memory.)

Finally, I was out of house arrest and happy to be free and on a ship again. I love ship sailing and riverboat steaming! So ended my Myanmar police encounter.

Like some other encounters, to this day I do not understand the motivation for my apprehension or detainment at Mergui. I can speculate that it was for my protective custody because the central government did not control the boondocks. There might have been guerilla or bandit activity that that officer was simply afraid for me and would not want to try to explain to the United States if anything untoward happened to me. This is pure speculation.

뻋

The Venezuelan police encounter in 1966 was on a frontier at a passport control guardhouse between Venezuela and Columbia. Near the Colombian frontier I visited a mission compound. I never crossed the border there, having had my fill of Colombia a year and a half before.

The bus back to Caracas, Venezuela, was stopped at a checkpoint. To my dismay, the police indicated for me to bring my pack with them into the guardhouse—as the bus rolled away to Caracas. Detained and stranded again!

As all these police encounters, I had no idea what on earth was going on; why me? An interrogation began in very halting English as I pretended, "*No spica da Espanol.*" I did not consider this a lie, as my Spanish was as halting as his English.

I have read it is harder to conceal knowledge than it is to conceal ignorance. Somewhere along I made the mistake of replying to something in Spanish and the official caught it. "Ah ha! You lie! You do speak Spanish!" He soon found out my fluency was too minimal for interrogation. His questioning dragged on.

There was great concern about my age and again I made a ghastly mistake. I replied, "Forty! As you see there in the passport!" He smirked, "Ah ha—but it says you are forty-one!" Only then did I remember my recent forty-first birthday. I had totally forgotten my own birthday!

My interrogator judged this apparent deception as strong evidence that I was lying because he believed that people do not forget their own birthdays or age. But that was no lie. I had a busy life and simply forgot to notice.

The police went on about how I admitted not giving my correct age and repeated that my passport said I was forty-one years old. I could not understand this overwhelming emphasis on what I considered a minor detail and asked why such interest. At first they ignored my question, but then it came out: Neither the passport photo nor I appeared that old. *Then* I lied.

It is true that Latin American women are of only two classes: a few upper-class women who, as far as I could see in my two years there, did absolutely nothing but eat and gossip. They had the lower-class Mestizo maids to do all the housework. The Mestizo women lived such hard lives that by their twenties, they appeared to be in their forties. The upper-class women appeared to age nearly as early, perhaps from sheer indolence.

So I explained, "But American women have all those machines to do the work so they stay young looking! Plus we have all sorts of cosmetics and beauty parlors to keep young looking!" Now I had observed many Latin women using much heavier cosmetics than American women in general, but these men seemed not to recognize my exaggeration. Whether it was this lying explanation as to why I did not appear to be in my the forties, that the last bus was leaving for Caracas and they did not want to jail me overnight, or that they had simply satisfied their purpose for that long interrogation, they let me go for the bus to Caracas.

The next day when I read a newspaper in Caracas, the mystery was solved. The paper told of a nationwide woman hunt for a twenty-six-year-old American brunette who had engineered the escape from jail of a leading Communist, possibly by bribing officials. Moreover, this brunette woman wore her hair in coronet braids!

Details of my Florida mistaken identity incident flooded my memory. I thought if I were trying to evade police, the first thing I would do would be to cut off such an identifying hairstyle, get a bottle of bleach for my hair, and get out of the country as soon as possible. Surely, that must have occurred to the police, too. My being so close to the frontier was another suspicious factor, except for the incongruous fact that I was headed *into* and not *out* of the country.

I heaved a huge sigh of relief for being let go from this police encounter and for having figured out the probable and ostensibly well-justified reason for this one.

This was the last police encounter I ever experienced abroad and it mirrored the first at home in that it was a case of mistaken identity based on distinctive hairstyle. If this were a novel, this account would make good closure for police encounters—and it almost did—but there was one more encounter, almost at home, in which I actually spent the night in a jail—a final time—at my own request.

බ—ග

The setting was the Hopi reservation in New Oraibi, Arizona, on Third Mesa.

Are the reservations considered "home" to Native American people who are United States' citizens? Are the reservations part of "our land," when they have the status of "domestic dependent nations"? Their geo-political status has many confusing inconsistencies. But I was arguably "in the United States," so I think of this incident as occurring "almost at home."

That Hopi reservation in Arizona is entirely surrounded by a much larger Navajo reservation. I had gotten to New Oraibi by a star mail route and intended to return with the same carrier in a very short while.

I had a package to mail to myself, so I parked my pack and a large purse at the door in order to take out my billfold to pay the postage. I could not have been in the post office for more than five minutes. When I came out to retrieve the pack and purse to take the star carrier leaving in a few minutes—they were gone.

Stolen!

This reality conflicted with what I had read or had been told. As a culture, Hopis do not steal.

The pack was dispensable, just a few old clothes I intended to replace immediately after this trip. The purse also had only one item of any value: my passport. There were no passport checks into or out of our domestic dependent nations, so that loss was not immediately crucial. But since I did not have a driver's license for identification purposes, I often carried my passport in the United States for identification. If it had not been for my passport, I think I would not have reported the theft. But for that, I had to let the mail carrier go and this time have a police encounter at my own seeking.

The station and jail were in the same building. I explained my plight to the two police officers on duty. At first, the noticeable difference in their size puzzled me but not for long. I knew Hopis to be relatively small in stature. Navajo, on the other hand, are quite large; the difference being similar to that between the Inupiat and the Thlingit or Athapascan indigenous peoples in Alaska.

The larger man said immediately, "That was no Hopi but a Navajo!" It turned out he was of the Navajo police force—each reservation has its own law enforcement agency; states and reservations do not cross jurisdictions— there to deal with Navajo malefactors, as there is much traffic of Navajos across Hopi land.

The two police agreed that the passport was a serious matter but also believed that whoever stole it would not be aware of its value for forgery. They thought that the thief might even toss the passport aside as useless to him. They got started on the machinery to recover my possessions, as only a short while had passed since the theft.

Unfortunately, that short while was long enough for the thief to get away with it. No trace ever turned up.

Meanwhile night was drawing on and there was no motel in New Oraibi then. What to do? Simple. Spend the night in jail—which I did.

The cell was equipped with clean sheets and amenities far better than many third world native hotels in which I had stayed. I cannot recall whether they also fed me or if I ate at some sort of diner in town.

My intention was that if no word had been received by the next day (and there wasn't), then I would take the star carrier back. Whether they had daily mail service I do not recall. Regardless, the Hopi police said waiting for the star route carrier was not necessary. They offered the use of their police car. They drove me to the reservation line, where a Navajo police car drove me out to their line, which was on a highway along which buses passed.

There I stood not long when I heaved a sigh of great relief upon seeing a Greyhound bus with a sign atop the windshield: New York!

Nowadays that would not mean anything. To begin travel along a route a passenger would have to be at a station and prepurchase a ticket. Back in those days, even transcontinental buses stopped on signal along the way.

As the driver pulled over, I flashed some money. "New York City, please," I requested.

"But where is your luggage?" the driver asked.

"I do not have any" was my reply.

"Not even a purse?" he asked incredulously.

"No," was my simple reply without explanation.

He shook his head but could not sell tickets that way. He told me that I needed to buy a ticket at the next station. As I approached the ticket window later, I overheard the driver telling how strange it was to go 2,000 miles without even a purse or any luggage at all—but fortunately I had the money.

Although this experience was not at all bad, I would have appreciated having a comb to tidy my braids. Yes, I could have bought a comb along the way and carried it in my other pocket. Instead, I was caught by the humor of taking a 2,000-mile trip with nothing but a billfold with "enough cash for it."

At home I replenished my personal things as necessary and notified the passport office of the stolen passport. They sent back a multipage form to fill out. One of those pages—the entire page—was for women to fill to list previous names, probably because of previous marriages! Women like Elizabeth Taylor might need so many spaces, but I was quite taken aback by it.

After only a few weeks I received my replacement passport. I never really expected to use it again and I never did go on any more extended trips as I had until then. I have gone on short tours to study something of interest, but I never have gone on a tour just to tour, though I no longer rule that out. I just have a penchant to study things. When in different countries for my studying, I also make a point now to tour their great tourist sites when I can, both natural and human-built wonders.

I was such a naive Philistine in my youth, throughout my early travels I sneered at some "tourist attractions" and missed them, decisions I now regret. Now I still hope to go abroad again to catch some, though with the time I have left now, it may be too late for me to do that. If I never get that opportunity I will still have gained much from my travels and I will have missed much, too. Such is life.

&~&

Thinking back, in spite of, or possibly because of that house arrest in Myanmar, I like Myanmar and its people so much! I can say the same about the Arabs and their countries and Turkey too, in spite of the police encounters. After all, in none of the encounters was I mistreated, just scared at the prospect of it. In the more than half a century since the night in the Hopi jail, I have never had another police encounter and hope never to have another.

All these many years later, when now I hear some people saying that they want to travel for adventure, I think, "Oh, how little do they know!" I am sure that some of the sweet experiences I have enjoyed, such as the sunrise over the Danube or seeing Zaccheus' tree in Jordan, are not the kind of adventures most people have in mind when they voice envy of adventurous travel as I have had.

Many people are not aware of the price—emotional, not monetary—that this sort of travel can require. Some of these memorable encounters were indescribable pleasures, but some were sheer horrors. I think most people simply would not pay but instead take the next plane home.

It was partly in hopes of finding some way for countries to provide more than just the barest survival for citizens that I went abroad in the first place. Needless to say, by the time I was on the Hopi reservation, I had never found it. But I am a little kin to Ann Frank in optimism—I still believe there *could* be (and certainly ought to be) such a world. Like Martin Luther King, I may not, most likely will not, live to see such a day, but—I have a dream, too: That some day such a day and better world will come.

STUDY QUESTIONS

1. The author states, "Crucial to my code of ethics, I never lie—never." Then she lied to serve what she claimed was a greater purpose.
   - What was the greater purpose? Did the purpose justify the lie?
   - Does the author sound credible that she did not want to get "the United States in trouble" during the money-changing episode, or is this a self-serving rationalization?
   - Should consideration of potential consequences of an act be taken into account when choosing a course of action?
   - What values were evinced by her course of action? Did the author's lying appear to "hurt her so," as she claimed?

2. Conflicting values often coexist in an individual's value system.
   - List and discuss examples from the chapter of conflicting values that coexist in the author's value system.
   - Does evidence exist in the text that indicates a conflict between stated values and demonstrated actions?
   - Was the author's self-perception consistent with her actions?
   - In cases where actions are inconsistent with stated values, does that indicate disingenuousness? If not, what else might it suggest?

3. The author said, "As all these police encounters, I had no idea what on earth was going on; why me?"

- Do you think that the author was actually ignorant of the reasons?
- If the reason was truly protective custody, why would the authorities not discuss that with the author?
- Given the historical context and evidence from the author's statements, what do you think were the reasons?
- Compare the author's claim of terror with her own account of her mood during the encounters. Did her actions during the encounters evince terror?
- Are any unspoken attitudes and values evinced by the pattern of detentions and the author's actions during the events?

4. After Intourist put her on a train for Moscow, the author assumed that she was out of their "clutches." When she saw a man carrying a placard with her name, she had paranoid thoughts that this might be the KGB. She admitted he might be an Intourist guide, but "assumption that I need help without my asking for it always did and still does infuriate me."

- Based on the author's knowledge of the situation, do you believe the claim about paranoia, or do you think that the author may have known the identity of the guide all along, but wanted to evade him and/or shunned his help because of her being infuriated?
- What unacknowledged feelings might underlie such sensitivity to being offered help?

5. The author claims, "Having been scrupulously law-abiding in my past."

- Was the author's behavior in the Moscow Intourist incident consistent with her self-perception of being law abiding? Cite other examples in the text that support or refute her self-perception.
- Discuss the hypothesis that the author was law abiding except when she judged laws or rules to run contrary to her beliefs about what made sense or was just. Cite specific examples.
- Discuss the legitimacy of claiming personal characteristics based on an idiosyncratic definition of terms instead of widely accepted definitions of those terms. Is this disingenuous, fraudulent, or inescapable due to the nature of language and self-perception?

6. In describing the process of getting a replacement passport, the author expressed surprise that the form included an entire page for listing previous names.

- Does this claim seem sincere or disingenuous? Why?
- What message was the author conveying about herself and her values by the choice of Elizabeth Taylor as an example in this passage?

7. The author says of the Agean Sea, "The water was so light and bright I could not understand why Homer wrote of it as wine-dark."

  - Discuss reason(s) you think might explain Homer's choice of words.

8. The author attributed the Canadian Mounted Police encounter to racial profiling.

  - What obvious situational factors were described by the author that would explain other reasons why the officer might have stopped?
  - Given the stated situation, is it possible that the officer stopped for reasons that are directly opposite of those hypothesized by the author?

Two

ALASKA, 1957–1960

Alaska was the last frontier of the United States. In the late 1950s, living there struck me as strange compared with life in the lower forty-eight. In some respects, it was similar to some foreign countries, such as British compounds in colonial India or some army bases in other countries. In fact, our compound *was* formerly a naval base.

Sitka, in southeast Alaska, is nestled on the west side of Baranof Island, flanked on the east by majestic snowcapped mountains and on the west by the calm waters of Sitka Sound and the sloping Mount Edgecumbe, an inactive volcano. The Indian River runs along next to Sitka and empties into its excellent harbor. Being the last ice-free harbor in Alaska, during World War II the United States established a naval base at Sitka. After the war the base was turned over to the United States Public Health Service for a large native hospital used mostly to treat tuberculosis, a scourge among natives at that time. In addition to the hospital, a native boarding high school was established.

As a result, the island experienced a significant influx of medical staff, teachers, students, and administrative personnel. The navy influence on housing structure remained. Single teachers and nurses were housed in the former Bachelor Officers Quarters (BOQ), while the enlistee barracks became the student dormitory. Another building that had lower rent housed non-professional staff members. These tended to be natives from around Alaska. But we did have a few teachers who were natives. They, too, had been assigned to the low-rent dormitory. This place had smaller rooms, but the chief distinction was that it was far less convenient because all teachers ate at the dining room in the teachers' dormitory about a mile distant from this housing. I protested this apparent segregation.

The former naval administration building was remodeled for use as the school. There was a road and one motor vehicle on our island. A free shuttle bus continuously circled between the two dorms, post office, school, hospital, and family housing. A free ferry service made frequent runs over to Sitka.

Students, teachers and hospital staff were in our compound from ice break up in late May until freeze up in September. The road ended no more than two miles in either direction from town along the coast. We were surrounded with the great temperate sub-Arctic spruce forest, impenetrable because of its density and the danger from bears. There was no road on the inland side of town. Usually only hunters ever ventured into the forest from that direction.

In Sitka a taxi served the airport and a hotel. There were two or three other automobiles, although I could not understand why. The town was too small to need vehicles. There must have been also another freight vehicle for crossing the channel besides the ferry, but somehow I never saw it.

For anyone familiar with only cities in the lower forty-eight, an entire town and off-shore island installation with only three cars and a shuttle bus is hard to imagine!

సంఅం

Sitka had only limited contact with the outside world at that time. One daily flight arrived from Juneau, Alaska, at about 10 a.m. and returned to Juneau at 2 p.m., weather permitting.

Telephones still did not connect directly to long distance. Instead, when we dialed, messages went by radio via the Coast Guard using a Federal Aviation Administration (FAA) tower located in Sitka. I did not understand the relationship of Coast Guard and FAA. Since we dialed a local exchange, at first I did not realize that for long distance I was somehow connected via radio.

Besides the daily flight to Juneau, our supply ship, the *Susitna*, came up from Seattle every other Friday. I thought of it as our umbilical cord, supplying us with food and all the necessities of our daily living. Of course, the Alaskan natives had made out very well on their own for thousands of years before the Russians got to them and later the Americans only the century before.

Going down to the dock every other Friday was a social event for many but I went only rarely. Once you have seen the big cranes reach into the hold and bring up a big crate of something, seeing it again is not that exciting anymore. The attraction was not as much seeing the cranes but watching other people standing around on the dock to pass the time of day as a social event. The post office served as a similar pastime, as people went daily to check their boxes for any mail from outside and then linger awhile to socialize.

I often thought of the difference between us, utterly helpless without the *Susitna*, and the self-sufficient native people there for so long before we arrived bringing our lifestyle with us. I realized that while native Alaskans were still more self-sufficient than we were, in the relatively short two centuries since outsiders arrived, they had become much more dependent on industrialized conveyances such as the *Susitna* and the Wien Airline that flew to all points around Alaska on demand.

At one point while I was at Sitka there was a sort of crisis at Barrow, 340 miles north of the Arctic Circle, our nation's northernmost community. The people had not caught a whale for food that year. Food supplies had to be flown in to them because their annual supply ship, the *North Star*, had already left to avoid the danger of being iced in until break up. (The village teachers at Barrow also used the *North Star* for their supplies. Imagine doing grocery shopping once a year!)

The Alaskan village schools had a radio. Teachers were assigned to call for a plane if someone got sick enough to need hospitalization. Pregnant women were usually flown out a week or two before their due date. Yet many were still delivered at home.

One Anglo teacher's labor came early. Her husband delivered the baby while listening to instructions from a doctor via the radio. This gained some notoriety in the small Bureau of Indian Affairs (BIA), but I supposed many of the native women's home deliveries had not even radio instructions to assist them. I wondered whether this were evidence that the native peoples were not valued as much as Anglo people were. Perhaps only the Anglo husband had access to a radio.

అ~ى

Revillagigedo Channel is the long water passage where the Alaska Marine Highway begins at the southeastern corner of the state and takes you almost all the way to Ketchikan, Alaska, the first town of any size. In the channel near Sitka was a spot known as the graveyard of ships because there was a huge rock on which many ships wrecked, as did the *Susitna* once.

The *Susitna*'s wreck was not disastrous in that there was no loss of life. The ship was able to limp to the nearest small Alaskan port for enough emergency repairs to get back to Seattle, Washington, for complete repair.

That was the only alternate Friday in my memory that the *Susitna* failed to make its Sitka delivery. I cannot recall whether I realized then or later how the wreck would affect our food supply.

The *Susitna* did not bring a wide variety of food in its hold each time like a gigantic shopping bag from the supermarket. Instead, bids went out for commodities, for example, for a three-year supply of turkeys that might come in on one trip, or a gigantic supply of potatoes on another trip. The lowest of three bids won the contract. The process takes a long time and a lot of planning. We could not just pick up a telephone, place a rush order for some commodity and receive it on the next delivery.

While the *Susitna* was not destroyed in the wreck, she took on water in the hold. We lost a huge shipment of fresh eggs. Our remaining precious supply of eggs had to be rationed for quite a long while, hospital patients getting first priority by doctor's prescription. How different can you get with the only way to obtain an edible egg being by a doctor's prescription! But most of us never ate another fresh egg for two years.

The cooks offered us a dried-egg concoction. After a few bites we stuck to cereal and pancakes. Next, they tried to use the dried eggs to make for a dip for French toast, but the taste was so bad that I preferred to just do without eggs.

Of course, the dried eggs were used in cooking, for example, to make pancake batter. That masked the unpleasantness. But for years, even knowing that the bread had been dipped in fresh whipped eggs, I could not tolerate the thought of eating French toast.

When the *Susitna* finally brought in fresh eggs, we did great celebratory feasting. Not omelets—but sunny side up so we could see that the eggs were whole, not beaten from some dried stuff.

సౌ౼౫

Just because we had no eggs for a while did not mean we suffered food scarcity. Quite the contrary. The BOQ dining hall had a cafeteria line. The meals were excellent and unlimited. A flat fee was deducted from our pay so that we never felt any financial strain to go back for additional helpings. And we did!

As months passed, I realized I was eating much more than my normal lower forty-eight intake. Everybody else ate a lot too!

Mealtime was teachers' social time, so we talked about everything including the unexpected phenomenon that we were all eating so much but not gaining weight. One conjecture was that it was psychological: There we were with only our small enclave away from normality, so we ate to prolong the table talk time as opposed to spending time in our dorm rooms in solitude. Another conjecture was that we ate because it was there for the taking. We may have been inclined to eat more because we did not have to trouble ourselves to do the food preparation or clean up and because additional portions were available at no additional cost. We might have geared our appetite to availability. That would explain additional eating, but not explain not gaining weight.

A different conjecture was that the phenomenon was physiological. Perhaps metabolic rates might be altered due to the change in day and night lengths. We ruled out climatic explanations having to do with cold per se because Sitka winters were never any colder than, say, New York winters.

By contrast, however, many, if not most, lower forty-eight states get hot in the summertime. While in Alaska we experienced sweater weather—occasionally heavy-coat weather—all summer long. Would the constant cooler temperatures trigger a body's need for more food or food higher in fat content?

The native peoples who also ate at the same table with us had not experienced any climatic changes, but they ate enormous meals also, even more than we did, if that was possible. Yet we never got fat.

I was some anxious that on my return to the lower forty-eight my body would be so accustomed to large amounts of food that I would feel hungry if I reduced my caloric intake to previous levels, or become obese if I continued eating large, but no longer necessary, amounts. I need not have worried. Almost at once I noticed that my post-Alaska appetite lessened from Alaska days back to my typical pre-Alaska appetite.

I still do not know whether our increased appetites in Alaska were caused by psychological or physiological factors.

৵৶

On a two-week summer vacation from school, I had flown to Anchorage, Alaska, on a regular commercial flight, air travel being the only means of transport at that time. From Anchorage, I took the Alaskan Railroad to Denali and later to Fairbanks. That train trip was most remarkable for its stunning scenery, both close up, with its mostly flattish terrain, and for the snow-covered Denali Mountains visible from the train for miles and miles across the plain.

The train would stop occasionally to allow passengers to disembark for picture taking before continuing the ride. Occasionally the train would stop for two or three hunters who had made arrangements to be picked up there.

An ingenious feature of the trip occurs at the halfway point. There the track divides as eastbound and westbound trains meet. Crews from trains traveling in each direction get off and exchange trains. In that way, each crew only goes halfway, so that each gets back home every day.

After my stopover in the park, I re-boarded the train a few days later to continue on to Fairbanks, from where I again flew, this time by Wien bush plane to Barrow. The bush plane was the same kind as the one that flew between Sitka and Juneau, with which I was familiar. Instead of our familiar two rows of seats for about a dozen passengers, though, this one had a single row of seats removed to make room for a load of lumber planks.

The real adventure that day was not in the flight but at the Fairbanks airport before take-off. The plane revved up, almost ready for take-off, when a bread truck zoomed across the tarmac. The pilot stopped the engine to load ordinary loaves of bread on top of the planks. The bread truck pulled away and we were revving up again when *another* truck zoomed up to the plane. This time they loaded three or four hangers of dry cleaning which were hung among us three or four passengers.

Imagine getting one's loaf of bread and dry cleaning delivered by air from about five hundred miles away! That was life in Alaska back then; I do not know what life is like there a half century later.

৵৶

The Wien pilot cheerfully called out for us when we crossed the Arctic Circle. I knew that for eighty-two days between May tenth and August second the sun would not go below the horizon or rise above the horizon from November eighteenth through January twenty-fourth in winter. Still no amount of book learning could prepare me for the actual experience of this phenomenon as I hiked along the coast of the Arctic Ocean.

Instead of appearing to traverse the sky from east to west, the sun revolved in a little circle overhead as though twirling atop an invisible pole. From the semicircular path, determining directions is easy. With the circling sun, I lost all sense of east-west or even north-south direction or orientation. Even the rule of having ocean to the north and tundra to the south did not appear to hold.

Despite being disoriented in space, being lost was impossible for the shore was only a few feet wide between ocean and tundra. I also observed that the ocean there seemed to be tideless. The width of the sand shore never varied.

Besides the space disorientation, I experienced time disorientation. Slogging several miles through sand is slow business and I soon literally could not tell if it was, say, 2 a.m. or 2 p.m. Even my biorhythms that determined hunger and the need for sleep seemed to go askew.

The experience of time and direction disorientation persisted only during the few days I spent in Barrow. Back in Fairbanks, my orientation returned.

&⌀⌀

For someone whose long time hobby is hiking, I needed no excuse to hike along the shore of the Arctic Ocean. On this hike my destination was Point Barrow, the ultimate farthest north point of United States soil, some dozen miles beyond the town of Barrow.

Such ultimate points fascinate me, so I did not want to miss this one while in Alaska. Perhaps I am somewhat self-deceptive in denying that I travel for adventure, for why else to hike to some ultimate point or to hike at all? This hike was for the sheer joy of reaching the northernmost geographic point of the United States. In the limited time I had for my school break, I could only go to one. The thrill I experienced there made my entire trip worthwhile.

&⌀⌀

When I arrived in Alaska, I learned the very important reason for the high value placed on teaching English. Except for the two native teachers, we teachers were monolingual English and our textbooks were in English. Instead of the two languages that I expected, Eskimo and Aleut, there were four other languages commonly spoken: Thlingit, Athapascan, Haida, and Tshimshian. How else could subjects such as biology, history, or math be taught to a class made up of so many different language speakers unless we had a common language?

To enter the high school, students had to be fifteen years old and have passed grade eight. By then they were fluent in English. In fact, the chief function of the village grammar schools was to teach English, with other subjects being a secondary goal.

I had heard rumors of harsh measures to force English on students "kidnapped" into BIA schools, including punishment for speaking their native tongue. I experienced no such thing. Possibly back in past dark ages these sorts of abuses might have occurred, but never then and I am sure not since, in any school.

Many native schools were not BIA affiliated, but missions. Many people did not draw distinctions. I cannot speak from experience about the mission schools since I only worked within the BIA structure. But any "forcing" was only by requirement and not by harsh method in my experience. I laud those teachers in the village schools. They did a very good job!

As for forcing boarding schools on native children, orphans of elementary school age were often compelled into boarding schools. At the high school age, no. To enter Alaskan native high schools, eighth graders had to take standardized tests. At Sitka we had a 750-bed dormitory. Only the 750 top applicants gained acceptance. Applying was not compulsory. Even the most top-scoring eighth graders, or their parents, could refuse to apply or decline acceptance. But that rarely—never to my personal knowledge—happened.

Native Alaskan parents, like most parents in general, are not stupid. Nearly all always want their children to get an education and are willing to make great sacrifices for them to do so.

We had informal standing orders never to question, for example, an occasional blonde-haired student who might be the result of bi-racial parentage, or informal adoption by native parents of an Anglo student who had no high school available. Sometimes Canadians left their children with American relatives or friends for the purpose of school not then available on the Canadian side. I understand that is no longer the case.

Considering the practical necessity of requiring all native children to learn and receive instruction in English, sometimes the teachers' table talk wondered whether if, in a few generations, the native peoples might forget their native languages and customs. We debated the ethics of having high school for native children at all since if they lived their simple, traditional lives in the villages, hunting and fishing for their living, they might not need the education we were providing. Would the lifestyle that we were teaching so spoil them that they might become dissatisfied with their traditional life yet never quite fit in the more modern world either?

I think most of us realized—or rationalized—that life was quickly going that way regardless of our concerns. Who could tell what the future would be like? We could only hope to widen their knowledge and provide more choices. Here we were, a bunch of Anglo teachers, doctors, and nurses, tending to their needs, essentially reinforcing or creating dependency. If any of these students were ever to become doctors, nurses, and teachers in order to return to their villages as leaders, they needed the opportunity to study a standard high school curriculum.

On the other hand, such a tiny minority of our graduates would go on for professional training that we wondered whether educating so many might be a waste of money. But then, how many students of any high school graduation class in the lower forty-eight actually continue to higher education, or *can*? We believed in the rationale that besides that small elite that might achieve a higher education, we must educate the majority of students for citizenship since they will be voting and such voters would be better informed, better for the state or nation, if more educated.

I am not so certain that citizenship education has worked out in practice, but then who wants to risk trying to get by as a nation of illiterates? Every advanced nation of the world puts a high priority on education. We teachers were, as evinced by the great sacrifice we made to teach there, committed to the goal with our very lives, even if we sometimes wondered whether the kind of education to which we were committed best suited the needs of our students.

Another element for me, though I do not recall any table talk about it is: Which of us has the wisdom to tell just what education is most needed and what kind is the best for any given child? Who among us can predict what the future holds for any given child as an individual or for any given society into which somehow this individual must "fit"?

I noticed after a few months that tolling of the Russian Orthodox Church bell signaled that there had been a death and that people were to gather—almost immediately—for the burial. On remarking about an immediate burial in contrast with the expected two or three days of mourning first, others gave me a surprised look. I had not noticed that there being no funeral parlor, the dead had to be buried very quickly after death.

Burial in the earth was difficult there since permafrost existed only about a foot or so under the surface. In the north, with frozen ground prohibiting burial for months but still with no embalming services available, the dead were stored frozen in a back room of trading posts until the earth thawed enough for burial. I did not observe this myself but was told so and it sounded plausible.

How else to dispose of the dead? Not cremation, for though in our town and all the way to the Yukon there was enough timber for that, north of the Yukon there was not. Still, cremation was not the custom.

Before first contact with the outside, Eskimo custom in a vast, sparsely populated territory was to leave a corpse on an ice floe. Missionaries were influential in stopping that method of disposing of the dead.

Occasionally a student would mention quite casually that his or her father had killed a man in the lower forty-eight and had come to Alaska to escape the law. The student would have come to the school after the parent married a native woman and settled there.

After hearing one such comment for the first time, I broached the subject in our table talk. Other teachers said the scenario was quite common, not just among our students but Alaska in general for two main reasons. One was that most states had no interest in pursuing any suspect up there. I thought state-side police might have shrugged if the crime were only a drunken brawl that got out of hand and maybe the loser was an unsavory character, too, who "got what was coming to him." Not to pursue persons suspected of major violent crimes surprised me.

Another reason for fleeing to Alaska to escape the law from the lower forty-eight was that it really was the frontier, a territory and not a state until the last year I was there. Even Sitka and Juneau looked like frontier towns of the westerns movies and television dramas. Stores were still made of wood, as were the sidewalks. The medium of exchange was silver dollars as much as it was paper dollars. Because Alaska was still a territory, law enforcement was the responsibility of a U.S. Marshal, although very rarely the Coast Guard sometimes jailed Saturday night drunkards in the brig of its cutter stationed there. The marshal's territory extended from his headquarters in Juneau all the way down the panhandle of Alaska as far as British Columbia, Canada, and possibly north of Juneau, too. Comprehensive law enforcement meted out by a single person over such a vast area was simply impossible.

Still, Alaska never seemed like a lawless place to me. At least I never had the idea that it was or needed any more law and order than already existed. We certainly did not need the extensive, highly organized police system found in most large cities.

In an area with such scattered population centered in very tiny villages where everybody knows everybody else and is probably a relative, there just is not much lawbreaking, especially with not many written laws on the books.

Even if smugglers wanted to take advantage of the vast, unguarded lands, what was there to smuggle and how would they dispose of the contraband?

I was told something else about the laxity of law enforcement in Alaska. Much of what might be considered crime in the lower forty-eight simply goes unreported in Alaska, for example, brawls getting out of hand in which one of the combatants is killed. The body is just dumped in the bay, so I was told, and nothing more comes of it.

I asked, if there were a wife and children surviving the victim, would they just leave unreported the loss of someone crucial to bring in enough fish to feed them? The answer I heard was that someone else would quickly be found to provide for the family.

In addition, Eskimos and other Alaskan indigenous groups traditionally share fishing and hunting catches for food (they do not share the furs in the same way) with any fellow tribal members who do not have a provider to share in the work of the fishing or hunting.

So Alaskans did not see much point in reporting the death of a missing husband suspected to have been killed to the marshal. Reporting could never bring the person back. I gathered that sort of reasoning or (in)action applied to both Anglos and natives. I do not vouch for the truth of this version of "life in Alaska," but the telling of the tale seemed widespread. Was it possible that the storytellers exaggerated the facts to impress this naive listener? Perhaps.

☙❧

Of the many minor oddities of Alaska, one was that money was not as common a medium of exchange as in the lower forty-eight.

One Saturday in Sitka, I saw one of my students hesitating at the door of the only store there that had men's clothing. He asked me to help him get a suit. I knew nothing about how to buy men's clothing but went into the store with him. Fortunately, in this instance, although normally I am such a staunch advocate of choice, there was no real choice: Only one suit fit him well. He looked very sharp and I said as much. Deciding to take the suit, he reached into his pocket, I assumed, to bring out a billfold with paper bills to pay. Not so. Instead, he brought out a very small leather pouch and opened its top. The proprietor brought out a scale from under the counter and a piece of thin paper about the size of an old-time roll-your-own cigarette paper. He put the paper on one pan and slowly poured from the tiny sack until the balance—gold dust!

Neither of them apparently found paying with gold dust noteworthy in the least, but my eyes popped wide. I did not comment on it then but later during table talk, the others said many students' parents gave them, if they had any, a pouch of gold dust for expenses the school did not provide.

The suit-purchasing incident made me wonder about how money in general, with no banks to process it, operated there. I saw that barter could work as in the case I witnessed, but how did the proprietor deal with the gold dust?

Sitka had a bank, but out in the villages certainly not. Were larger amounts of gold dust flown by Wien and then by other flights to Seattle for banking there? What would be done with it then?

I suppose nowadays credit cards must have replaced gold dust, just as plastic is found in the boondocks of third world countries now. What a change from bartering gold dust to electronic transfer of funds, then to now.

The purpose of my travels was to broaden and deepen my understanding of the customs of sociopolitical groups more so than to meet individuals per se. My observations of individual interactions, such as in this gold dust incident, gave me a glimpse of their culture in an unexpected way.

ॐ

A great thirst to experience our last frontier and the far north had drawn me to Alaska. Not that I had experienced all that much, but I had experienced enough to leave. By the end of the third year, I knew I had to get on with the next stage of my life. My immediate plan was to go abroad again to the then-Communist empire or Soviet Union. But first, I was going home. Home!

The Seattle-Alaska connection was also key in getting in or out from the lower forty-eight. Now, there are many direct flights stateside to Anchorage but then, all flights went first through Seattle. Getting from Sitka to Juneau to Seattle to anywhere else involved in every case, I think, overnight in Seattle.

Federal agencies put its employees up in a Seattle YWCA hotel, which also housed men. That has probably changed now, too. But since that was the hotel we knew in Seattle, when we traveled on our own, everybody I knew used the YWCA, going and coming.

As I left Sitka, I stayed another time in that Seattle YWCA. I went to a nearby grocery store to revel in this element of ordinary American lifestyle. I had not consciously missed grocery stores in Alaska. In fact, Sitka has a grocery quite like a stateside supermarket. Because of the BOQ meal service, I had never shopped for groceries there.

In the market, I saw boxes of fresh milk. I like milk well enough but not especially fondly and had not consciously missed having fresh milk. We had plenty of dried milk made up, which turned out much better than those miserable dried eggs. Yet seeing those cartons triggered a craving for real, fresh milk. I drank right from the box as I browsed.

Suddenly—to my surprise—the box was empty! I had drunk the whole quart! Now that I recognized my unwitting hunger for milk, I got another box to sip back in my room. At the checkout counter, I showed the empty box and full one.

"Just out from Alaska, eh?" the young woman giggled, "How long were you there?"

"Three years" came my reply.

The clerk told me that many people coming out from Alaska did as I did; drinking the milk straight from the box right there in the store.

Thus I discovered that I had acted just as many coming out of Alaska did!

ॐ

Is Alaska still a frontier? I think that I arrived just at the waning moments of frontier, with statehood right around the corner.

Alaska joined the Union in the last year that I was there. I voted in favor of statehood in that election. Since I left a few months later, I do not know how daily life might have changed for individual because of the change.

We human beings have managed to survive in the most challenging environments found on the planet, from the frozen tundra to the arid deserts to the thickest rain forests, for millions of years. But the powerful nature of recent technology developed in only the last century of our existence is frightening. Still, that technology comes from the power of the human brain—to replace the power of human muscles!

The only hope I see is if we redirect that same brain power to the search for non-destructive technologies. We need to focus collective human willpower to the purpose of using technology to advance abundance of life, prosperity for the human family, and long-term planetary preservation.

Will we see in time enough and have the will enough to change our lifestyle for the sake of future survival of our whole planet? Is my thinking that this is a matter of survival a pessimistic or a realistic view?

Can we do it? Probably.

The more important question is, *will* we do it? Possibly.

I can only hope.

STUDY QUESTIONS

1. The author states that she protested the apparent segregation evinced by one native teacher being assigned to the less-expensive living quarters.
   - What action do you think she took to express her protest?
   - Can you think of reasons other than segregation that might have caused the native personnel to be assigned to the more distant living quarters?

2. An Anglo teacher's husband had radio instructions to deliver their baby, while natives delivered without instruction. The author wondered, "whether this were evidence that the native peoples were not valued as much as Anglo people were."
   - What reasons other than being less valued might explain why native people got no radio instruction for birthing?

3. The author describes gleaning a great deal of knowledge about Alaska and its peoples from participating in talk around the dining table.
   - Compare and contrast this table talk with the symposia of Athenaeus and Aristotle.

Three

ROADS TRAVELED

My extensive travels have taken me to every one of the fifty states of the United States and to many other countries abroad. I am not sure when my fascination began, but roads of all kinds appeal to my imagination and stimulate my curiosity.

Where does the road lead? Any new place was of great interest to me. Even familiar, often-traveled roads fascinated me. Half a century later, I thrill at the thought of travel along roads, whether they be on land, sea, or air.

≈≈≈

The Pan-American Highway is a system of roads spanning 16,000 miles extending from Fairbanks, Alaska, to the southern tip of Chile. The system is more a concept than a single highway. Two of the most famous sections of the Pan-American system are the Alaska-Canadian Highway, affectionately known as Alcan, and the Inter-American Highway.

Some say that at the northernmost end, the Pan-American begins in Circle Hot Springs, Alaska, only fifty miles south of the Arctic Circle. In the late nineteenth century, miners erroneously named the town thinking that the location was much closer to the circle. Now thanks to the trans-Alaskan pipeline, the Dalton Highway allows drivers the option of starting their trip along the Pan-American even further north, from the shores of the Beaufort Sea in Deadhorse, Alaska.

The Richardson Highway, in place for decades before the Alaska Highway opened, is the route south from Fairbanks to Delta Junction, Alaska. From Delta Junction the Alcan spans another 1,522 miles, winding southeasterly through Alaska, through Canada's Yukon Territory to British Columbia.

Engineered during World War II by the U.S. Army Corps of Engineers, the Alcan traverses what was then unmapped wilderness so rugged that completion was considered an impossible feat. Beginning as a muddy, twisting, single-lane trail fit only for trucks and bulldozers in the 1940s, now the highway is mostly smooth going all the way. Today the Alcan still provides the only land route to Alaska.

No official route for the Pan-American Highway is defined in Canada or the lower-forty eight because with so many other pre-established roads, you can select any convenient route to Mexico as you travel through those countries. The only gap in the system is Darien Gap between the Panama Canal in Panama and northwest Columbia.

The Inter-American Highway, 3,400 miles long, connects border cities of the United States to Panama. The original route had two prongs in the United States. The eastern prong ran from Laredo, Texas, and the western prong from El Paso, Texas, through Mexico Distrito Federal (Mexico City), to Panama City, Panama.

Continuing south after Panama City, the route resembled not our usual image of a "highway," but a torturous road going on and on and *on* to the Nordic-style town of Puerto Montt, Chile, 944 miles north of Tierra del Fuego, Chile.

The Pan-American Highway concept was quite recent when I made the trek. Suggested at the Fifth International Conference of American States in 1923, the highway was supported and financed by Franklin Delano Roosevelt during his presidency. Nearly every bridge had a sign: built by the people of that country and the people of the United States.

I was vaguely aware of Roosevelt's great works in Latin America as part of the "Good Neighbor Policy." By extending roads into South America, we could more easily transport goods between North and South America.

When I was in Latin and South America, people told me stories they learned at school or from their parents about the pre-road days and the tremendous impact that the road had on life there.

I understood that the gap was passable by jeep but that would mean finding the way over roadless territory that included 125 miles of thick jungles, tortuous rivers, low but rugged mountains, and a vast, marshy swamp. Now I understand all but fifty-four miles of the road through the gap has been completed, but no commercial traffic crossed that area then or now.

Instead, small motor boats carried goods and passengers across Darien Gap, making brief stopovers along the way at isolated stores along the coast for the cigarettes and drinks. Larger freight went by ship. We made one longer stopover in a town, but that was not long, as the town was too small to support a hotel. The primary reason for stopping was to supply fresh movie reels and pick up the movies from the previous week to return to Panama City.

The people looked like images straight out of *National Geographic*, wearing G-strings in the village, but the non-native movie proprietor required patrons to wear clothing to enter the barn/shed that served as his movie theater.

I went into the theater more to see the people than the old-fashioned shoot 'em up western being shown. I wondered whether westerns were the only type films available or just the ones the natives preferred to watch.

As I recall, this leg of the journey took three days.

I had started the trip thinking that the Inter-American Highway must largely follow the route of the ancient Inca road system that went from Cuzco, Peru, as far north as Colombia and quite a way south, I think, nearly the entire length of the South American Pacific coast. Much of that ancient road system was built at very high altitudes. But no.

Numerous side roads do go up into and along the mountains and these were all considered parts of either the Pan-American System or the Inter-American Highway. Indeed, one stretch was *so* steep that it evoked the gasp that some fool Yankees had traveled that road for adventure. But the main route is nearly along the coast at lower altitudes.

I was not looking for treacherously steep roads merely for adventure, but once I accidentally found a stretch of the ancient Inca road near Machu Picchu, Peru, and I did travel along that a little way for pure adventure.

My first Fourth of July spent abroad found me in Ankara, Turkey. That year I completely forgot that the day was a holiday for me. That year, to mark the holiday, I planned my visit to Machu Picchu, a fortress city of the ancient Incas, in a high saddle between two peaks about fifty miles northwest of Cuzco. Even more than the great glory of the Inca ruins there, the greatest thrill for me was the one I had not even previously known about, that stretch of the Inca road.

The road crossed a tremendous chasm by a swinging bridge over what looked like a thousand-, or maybe two-thousand, foot drop on either side.

What possessed me to cross that bridge? I do not know. Maybe it was for a "fool Yankee" notion of thrill after all.

On backpack trips I had crossed such bridges—usually with a railing, but sometimes not—but never as long as this bridge and certainly never as high above a raging torrent far below.

Worse, I knew I would have to cross back!

But fool I was, cross it I did, and then I continued on for a short way. I would have liked to hike on for a long way, but fool or not, I never have gone farther away from base than a spot from which I was sure I could return.

That base was a real find, courtesy of some U.S. Peace Corps workers who had come from near and far in South America with the same yen as I had to experience this great world archaeological treasure. They had the advantage over me, having learned from previous Peace Corp volunteers about one of those roofless ruins having straw on floor and tacitly set aside for free camping for those in the know. An added bonus was our find that the hotel tacitly allowed us to use its facilities without charge, even for showers before 8 a.m.

People in this low-budget mode could either splurge and eat at the hotel or bring their own food, but there were no cooking facilities. This is no real hardship, as most of us did not mind much eating three cans of tuna a day with crackers and water. Except in South America we did not have tuna in cans. Instead, it was some bony, not nearly as good-tasting fish. But we ate what we could get and there were plenty of bananas and oranges. Whatever else we could come by we shared. I was glad I had bought some food up from Cuzco to add to the bounty.

I thought of the Inca road as a subsection, although totally disconnected, of the Pan-American Highway.

I traveled the Inter-American Highway and Pan-American road, in slow stages, all the way from El Paso, Texas, to Arica, Chile's northernmost city. I am still awestruck at the thought of it—without words to adequately describe the experience, just too much, too big!

Though a map could show the eyes and brain a representation, I submit that not until you have traveled the road personally can you begin to fathom the vastness of the distance or the astounding beauty of the vistas.

৯৩৬

One of the most ancient road systems I had the thrill to walk along was the Old Silk Road, the widespread network of caravan ways crossing Europe and Asia, extending all the way from the Mediterranean coast to old Cathay, the English name for China. In ancient times and the Middle Ages, this route served as an important means of business relations and cultural exchanges between East and West. I walked along a part of the route east of Samarkand, Uzbekistan, in the Soviet Union.

The Intourist program in Samarkand toured its wonderful ruins of blue mosques and madrasehs, or Qu'ranic schools, theological schools that focus on the study of Islam. The tour mentioned the Old Silk Road, but walking a distance on the route was not included in the plan.

To my way of thinking, there were two main attractions to Samarkand: the ruins and that route. Of the two, the route won hands down possibly because I was familiar with it from the Marco Polo account. Of course, it was never a "road"—unless in short stretches near towns—as much as a well-worn route overland across two continents. Not straight or direct, the route included many miles of variance for camel caravans to go from oasis to oasis.

This section was part of the longest part of the Silk Road used back when people thought that the great western sea was the end of the world. That evening, I headed out to experience a sort of semi-mystic imagination of it at its prime. At that point I found a pleasant, dusty path. Bright moonlight lit the night. Many people were going and coming, all intent on their business, not noticing or bothering with me. I wondered what businesses were keeping them out so late. Left to my romantic imaginings, I walked on for several miles in a sort of exalted mood, singing in silent joy—so heady to think walking directly on to China was possible!

The thought crossed my mind to try to find the road eastward of Samarkand that would continue the Old Silk Road, but this had not been mentioned by the Intourist guide. I had such longing to continue walking, for no doubt this would be a once-in-a-lifetime opportunity. I felt as if I could walk on indefinitely. Common sense demanded that I return.

Before I turned to head back, almost in the center of Samarkand it seemed, were those majestic mosque ruins that I had seen in the daytime. Now in the bright moonlight, the mosques were even more magnificent. The bright moonlight meant dark shadows too. This masked the ruin aspects so they seemed alive. Visions of sultans and harem dancing girls filled my imagination.

As I realized the time was very late or very early depending on how I looked at it, I reluctantly tore myself away from this peculiar communing with the Old Silk Road and the ruins of Samarkand to return to the hotel. I got back to the hotel in time for shower and breakfast. I supposed that day I would feel drowsy, but I did not at all.

If only for a few miles on a moonlit night, I had traveled along the most ancient and fascinating "road" on our whole globe in the history of human civilizations.

People hearing of my travels have asked me, "But what did you *do* while you are traveling to those unknown places?" I suppose most people do not comprehend my personal yen to walk along historic roads or see ancient sites. But for me, that all-night walk along the Old Silk Road by those ancient mosques remains one of the most memorable nights of my life.

⤚⤜

The first Roman road I walked was not until 1982 on my second trip to Israel. I took an all-day walk down the Old Roman Road from Jerusalem to Jericho. Jerusalem is twenty-three-hundred feet above sea level. Seventeen miles away, Jericho is thirteen-hundred feet below sea level, down near the Dead Sea in the area known as the wilderness. Who would ever choose to walk *up* in that hot desert sun? But what a thrill that walk was for me!

This is the very *same* road, I think, of the biblical route from Jerusalem to Jericho. Steep, Roman horse traffic but not chariots found it passable. But the Roman legions did not depend on chariots much though, did they? Most traffic then, as on the day I walked, was pedestrian.

I thought again of how what in ancient times was a mode of transport or travel, human feet, are now for a few of us, such as myself, just a recreation or sometimes, as for me on that day, a way to experience history in deeper fashion than speeding along a highway can afford.

That day's walk on the "real" road down from Jerusalem to Jericho and an hour or so wade through Hezekiah's Tunnel remain today the highlights of that second pilgrimage to Israel.

⤚⤜

In addition to desert oases, another factor that determined the routing of ancient roads were mountain passes. The king of mountain passes for the whole planet is the great Khyber Pass through the Hindu Kush mountain range connecting the northern frontier of Pakistan with Afghanistan.

While I was in Kabul, an emissary of the U.S. Embassy came to my hotel room to tell me about the cholera epidemic and offer immunizations at the embassy. Since I had not reported my whereabouts to the embassy, evidently border officials of various countries must report to them about the identity and whereabouts of travelers. How else did they know even the hotel I was in?

Nonetheless, the emissary also offered me a ride through Khyber Pass to Pakistan in a diplomatic car, telling me I would be disappointed in this fabled Khyber Pass, as it had not much to see at all. I turned down the offer for my preferred mode of "going with the people" by bus.

I still have difficulty grasping the idea that to go over a mountain pass in some places requires going *up*, sometimes to a very high point. The only lowness involved is by comparison to the even higher mountains around.

Going through Khyber was a two-day bus trip out of Kabul, the capital of Afghanistan, with an overnight the city of Jalallabad, Afghanistan near the top.

The pass has old, ruined, fort-like structures atop many hills. I was surprised to see hills within the pass. I could almost see a British officer or two leading probably some unit of sepoys.

Long before the British arrived—I was and am hazy about various conquerors and wars of world history—the area had been the scene of many invasions and the passage of several cultures on the way to India. I meant to study the history of Khyber Pass sometime but that time has not yet come.

The emissary was entirely wrong in predicting that I would be disappointed. People's judgments about boring or thrilling vary. I was deeply moved just being there.

இ⊷இ

Another memorable Andean Mountain pass I crossed lies between La Paz and Cochabamba, Bolivia, located on the continental Amazon lowland plain. At 8,500 feet, Cochabamba is not *that* low in elevation, except by comparison to La Paz's dizzying elevation of 12,000 feet above sea level.

We left by truck at four or five o'clock on a very cold morning. I had never seen any terrain as steep as Paso del condor, where it was snowing. I think at 16,500 feet, it is the highest pass in the world with a paved road over.

I had not learned the altitude of the Khyber Pass, but it was not nearly as cold and somehow I think not as high. Some of the Himalayan passes, the escape routes of Tibetan Dalai Lamas, are higher, I think, but no roads there allow truck passage.

After crossing the pass, we went steep down for the rest of the day.

First, I crawled out from under my sleeping bag, then shed my winter coat, scarf, and mittens. Next I exchanged boots for sandals. Then off came my warm, long nylon stockings, replaced by ordinary socks, then off came my sweater.

By the time we reached Cochabamba, a sleeveless summer dress and sandals were my attire. In just one day we had passed from snow and bitter cold—not even at the pinnacle of the Andes, peaks still towered high above the height of Paso del condor—to the warm valley floor.

My fellow passengers on the truck were very impressed first by the warm sleeping bag in which I was cocooned against the cold and then at how I was layered under it to allow for the temperature change. The native habit was to only layer two or three shawls that they shed as the temperature rose.

That ride was even more memorable than the Inter-American Highway rides because the road was even more narrow, winding, and precipitous. The locals refer to the road as down and up instead of east and west, for although it does go so steep up for a while out of La Paz, after the pass it is steep down for hours and hours. On return, I expected that we would travel steep up for many hours before the pass and then have a short zoom down into La Paz.

This characteristic caused me a troublesome mistake on the return. Having come over the same route earlier, I knew the cost, so held out exactly enough for return fare. When the driver indicated I should pay more, I was angry, not so much because the cost would be more, but because I thought he was cheating me—a first in all my travels abroad.

I felt my faith in humankind was being shattered. The poor driver did not have a command of English adequate to explain, but someone else did: The up journey costs double the down journey. Then, of course, I had to try to apologize for my mistake.

଺ఠ

Twice I traveled on non-roads just going along the plain. The first time was from Khartoum, Sudan, east to Asmara, Eritrea, and then the regular road through the Ethiopian capital of Addis Ababa.

When I inquired, I found the bus made the trip only twice a week. But there being a bus, I assumed this meant a road on which the bus would travel. When I boarded, I expected the typical third world rickety ex-school bus with ever so many passenger bundles and babies squeezed in. Taking its Islamic tradition more seriously than any other Muslim country, even Pakistan, this bus also observed strict segregation of women and men. The aisle, unlike what you would find in an ordinary western bus, was already crowded with older children, bundles, and passengers who had not gotten seats. To add to the confusion, while the women remained in their seats, men came forward to speak with their wives, creating even more traffic in the aisle.

What amazed me most about this bus trip was that on leaving the city of Khartoum, the road ended—period. The bus just drove on all day long across savannah-like terrain, with a view of mountains in the distance. There were not even ruts, except on occasion to show where previous buses had been. There may have been other traffic just beyond visibility driving across the savannah, but I do not recall seeing a single other motorized vehicle that whole day.

❦

The other non-road was not so literally a non-road. I was traveling around Brazil and the map showed the road ending at some boondock town, Rondonopolis, I think. But people had told me there was a road across Mato Grosso to Puerto Velho, Brazil, where I could get a boat from down the Rio Madeira from there to Manaus, Brazil, and eventually down the Amazon to Belem, Brazil. The way to go, they explained, was to wait at edge of town for a truck and pay whatever agreed upon. My advisers were right. The truck that stopped had a load of oil barrels, going to Puerto Velho.

Although it was a two- or three-day journey by truck across so many miles, there was literally no place else *to* go along this road, although there were two or three let-offs or pick-ups in the middle of nowhere, where I assumed, as it had been in Alaska, natives lived in cabins away from the road.

I do not recall what we did at lunchtime; maybe we just skipped lunch. In the late afternoon, the truck would stop at some ramshackle house in the wilderness. Then there would be something quite as I imagined frontier days here had been. The driver would take money from my hand—I never knew exactly how much. Then he hooked a hammock on porch posts as I unrolled my sleeping bag. I would have preferred a hammock too, to ease my snake anxiety, but then snakes could climb those posts, so maybe it made no difference.

Meanwhile the woman of the household would dispatch several children for various chores: to kill a chicken to be fried, to gather up a dozen eggs or so to be fried, an older daughter to peel—maybe first to dig?— potatoes to be fried, to put on water to boil for rice, and to prepare some starchy root vegetable, maybe boiled. Then we would eat.

In our three-day journey, I recall having essentially the same meal more each day. I recall coffee too. Then we would roll into sleep on the porch. Breakfast was rice, that root, and coffee. Then back to the barrels to continue our journey. Actually, it was surprisingly comfortable up there for me with my back against the truck cab.

Although a non-road on the map, the route appeared distinct because of its ruts. It crossed several streams. Mostly these were shallow; the truck just drove on through the water. Other places had two boards forming the crudest of bridges. I thought it must take great skill to hit those planks exactly enough to get across, but they always hit the mark. "They" because there were two drivers, one more like an assistant.

Twice we saw two or three natives wearing G-strings with painted faces. One group just happened to be near the road, apparently. The other group had something to trade and waited for whatever rare traffic might come, or perhaps it was a pre-arranged meeting. They had a parrot in a homemade cage. The driver bought it from them. I did not mind sharing the barrels with another person or two for short stretches, but was not looking forward to that parrot with me despite it being caged. Fortunately, the driver took it into the cab with him.

When we arrived at Puerto Velho, I was sorry to have this thrilling-to-me trip across the whole of Mato Grosso and half of Brazil end. I had been quite comfortable the whole way, except for some nervousness when we crossed rivers over planks. Even crossing rivers there was no real danger, for if the truck ran off the planks, the streams were shallow enough not to sink the truck and from atop the barrels, I had a safe vantage point. Otherwise the experience had been one of sheer enjoyment.

The driver came to say farewell. He told me his partner had not wanted to take me as he expected an American woman to be horrified at traveling that way; once underway there could be no turning back, no succor in case of emergency along the route of that almost endless road in the wilderness.

Contrary to their worries, he indicated high approval of my toughness to withstand the rigors of the trip. I had never been a bit of any sort of trouble to them. His enthusiasm gave me to wonder if perhaps I was the first American woman he had taken on that trip.

I did know that travel by boat was the usual mode of travel in Brazil because of the huge interior roadless areas, but thought travel over water would be much more expensive. I preferred to try the less-traveled mode about which I had heard by word of mouth. It worked for me.

పూలు

Back in simpler days, before the interstate network was built, I sometimes hitchhiked in the United States.

On one occasion, I arrived at the bus station in St. Louis, Missouri, just a few minutes after the bus to New York had departed. The next bus to New York was not scheduled for hours. Grrr!

Then the bus station was just two blocks from the bridge across our mightiest river, the Mississippi. I decided rather than just wait several miserable hours, I would try a lift, with the intention to stay close to bus stops along US Route 40. In addition to my customary, "I'm a lady!" I would request that any proffered rides take me as far as Terre Haute, Indiana, so I would not be stranded at a farm somewhere along US Route 40 as the bus rolled past.

I barely got to the bridge when a car stopped for me and assured me that he was going past Terre Haute. It was not until later that we mutually told our final destinations, mine along the Hudson River and his in Troy, New York.

So we rolled across US Route 40. I fell in love with that highway across the heartland of my own native land with its green farms and cities along that whole stretch. The interstate skirts the towns so one never gets that feeling of kinship with the people along the road or the sense that the road is part of some bigger entity and thus part of me or I a part of it.

I do not know where the driver turned off US Route 40 to turn north toward the Hudson River system and home. He pulled off only once or twice to nap. I napped along the way as was my custom on overnight bus trips. He dropped me at my door and refused to come in for a rest or sleep before going on to Troy, despite our not arriving until three o'clock in the morning.

I always meant to travel the entire length of the US Route 40. Extending farther west as the country expanded into the west, it was one of the first national roads, along with US Route 1 and US Route 9. But I never did. I have, however, been on it more than once, as it reaches from St. Louis all the way into California, on my way to San Francisco, by bus.

The interstate highway system has opened faster travel for tractor trailers and huge buses as well as millions of cars in the United States, but these roads do not yet have the patina of history going along with them as our numbered national roads do. In that respect, they are not as interesting.

I am glad to have traveled these historic US Routes when I did before they become as obsolete as the Silk Road and ancient Roman roads, when the flavor of their history was still there for the experiencing.

ॐॐ

The Roman, Incan, Pan-American, and Old Silk Road systems all accommodated primarily military and trade needs. The Alcan Highway project was pushed to completion to transport lend-lease war goods to Great Britain and the Soviet Union even before the United States' entry into World War II, but after we entered, war goods transport over that highway was stepped up even more. I saw that the great web of American highways also appeared to be primarily for transporting goods, with movement of people only a secondary objective, but I had not pictured my own country as so militaristic that it would build roads with military purposes as the primary objective.

During the rainy season of late 1966 in Brazil, I overheard an interesting remark that made me rethink that idea. I was out in the boondocks as usual, I have forgotten where I was headed; I may have been in Curitiba, Brazil. The bus often got mired in the sea of mud that was the unpaved road. When we got stuck, the male passengers put their shoulders to the bus to push until we could continue. (I was glad to be female!)

Though I was not fluent, Portuguese is very near to Spanish and I understood one remark perfectly. One of the straining men expostulated at the miserable road, "Why has the United States not fixed it?" I found like sentiments expressed by people everywhere in Latin America, blaming the United States for not ameliorating their problems.

Even when my fellow passengers realized that I was American, they often voiced blame as though hoping to educate me to the greedy imperialism of the United States. What surprised me was the reply from another man who was also pushing hard, "No, the United States will not fix this road because it is not a military objective." I felt very bad as I wondered if besides being mere greedy imperialists, we were also such a militaristic country that anything we do must have some military objective? That man's image of the United States was so opposite to my naively optimist image of the country of my dream, with liberty and justice for all, our own people and others in the world.

The man's remark got me thinking about the vast network of interstate highways just being built in the United States, the concept of President Dwight D. Eisenhower, the general before the president. If in back of his mind was that, like the Alcan, these highways would expedite transport of war goods "just in case," it seemed to me that overland travel would already be obsolete, replaced by air freight, by the time of any future war. As soon as any war hereafter even started—in this new nuclear age—it would already be too late to transport goods or troops.

&ᕗᕼ

Railroads, more precisely the trains that travel over them, have also captured my imagination and interest. Recall that I boarded the Tashkent Express at Moscow. Words fail me about that fabulous train ride. The distance north to south in the Soviet Union is as vast as our country from east to west.

As usual, "when words fail," I suppose now I will use quite a lot of them despite my claim that I have none. What I mean, of course, is that I recognize the impossibility of conveying my own mental images in words so that the reader will receive the same, or nearly the same, mental picture.

The Tashkent Express was comfortable, more so than my train or bus rides across the United States. Even though I rode third class, the wooden benches fitted my back well and never felt too hard. As on European trains such as the Orient Express and the train from Leningrad to Moscow, the aisle is not in the middle with two seats either side, but along one side of the car, with four nighttime and six daytime spaces and seats facing each other. This arrangement is more conducive to camaraderie and provides more legroom.

This train had a feature I had not seen before or since. A folding table for daytime use was situated between the facing seats. On the first night an attendant brought bedding, folded out two uppers berths, and folded the table back, creating two lower berths. The berths were not parallel to the sides as found in U.S. sleeper cars but situated across the compartment.

In the mornings the attendant folded away the bunks with bedding inside. In evening and morning—one of the great features of this train—he served tea from a big samovar, hot and good.

In Intourist hotels, the tea of the meal came with its coupon, so sugar and sometimes, if requested, lemon was included. But in "workers'" restaurants, sugar cost a ruble or so more, as did cream, or lemon if there was any. Tea was cheap but sugar cost as much as the tea.

On the Tashkent Express I think I recall that the tea came sugared. I do not recall if it was part of the ticket or if we paid a few rubles for the great service. Tea there was served in a glass sitting in a light metal holder with a handle. I wondered how the samovar made it that we could get the tea *hot* because elsewhere in the Soviet Union hot tea in a restaurant was never hot, only warm.

Passengers with enough rubles could go into first class for meals but most carried a supply of food with them. This was a reason I loved that train ride so much. Other places like the mosques and ruins, while fascinating, did not offer the opportunity to interact with the common people. The passengers were very friendly and hospitable. They shared their food with me despite my having none to share.

If I took some of the smilingly offered food, I would hold out some rubles as an offer to pay, which the passengers smilingly refused. Word of my presence rapidly spread to other compartments throughout the train. Soon a parade of people came to offer not only food but picture magazines: they must have realized that I was too limited in Russian to read! Some simply came to be seen and smile in what seemed to be honest delight at seeing an American.

Besides the food carried by passengers, at every stop women had good-looking food for sale. Passengers would buy more food, often two of each thing selected, then come to offer me the extra. I recall eating those four days and nights better by quite a bit than by coupon in the Intourist hotels. The flavor of the food may have been enhanced by the experience of enjoying it with people in good spirits rather than eating solitarily or with other English speakers there to witness Communism as I was.

This being third class, there was not as much opportunity to converse as there was in that first-class compartment overnight from Leningrad to Moscow where the young men spoke passable English. Sometimes this is a good thing. On occasion, I enjoyed merely observing the people around me, their actions unfiltered by their words. Silence eliminated the possibility of disillusionment. Being inclined to optimism and friendliness as I am, without specific evidence to the contrary, I tended to see that in others.

When I did find English speakers with whom to converse, I took up the opportunity to hear from the people about their views of Communism. On that train ride, regulated capitalism did not appear to be any better than Communism. In conversations with people whom I met in the Soviet Union, I always tried to point out some mitigations of the stereotype of unchecked power to exploit, such as the graduated income tax, but the arguments rang hollow even to me. I was aware of some instances where corporations received more in subsidy than they paid in tax and the gross discrepancies between the incomes of CEOs by comparison to say, janitors, with much of the top executives' income distributed in ways to avoid taxation.

I also saw that regardless of differences in religion, belief or non-belief, or ethnicity, we all appeared to share a mutual respect for humanity, finding that a good thing.

Hearing directly from the people on that train ride was such an excellent antidote to constant Intourist propaganda that I wondered why the Soviet Union all but refused to let tourists into third class to really meet and greet its people. I wonder, in this post-Soviet Union age, whether there still is such herding or watchfulness of tourists. Even then I think that the idea was not to watch us as much as to watch their own people, to prevent them from having enough contact with us that they would get ideas that might turn them against Communism.

At some point along the way, I realized that we had crossed from Europe into Asia. Though I had not noticed crossing the Ural Mountains, I saw camels from the window. The villages of dun-colored stucco and flat roofs looked more like desert homes found in Asian steppes than the more "ordinary-looking" villages amid green fields, pastures and low hills of Europe. Nearly every one of the dun-colored villages had a white minaret of a mosque visible above the housetops.

I assumed these mosques were relics of pre-communist time and no longer in much, if any, use. If I might have given the idea much thought, I might have assumed the same for Russian Orthodox churches also, but as those do not usually rise higher than other buildings of a town, none came to my awareness as the minarets did.

Today Uzbekistan is very much a part of "the Muslim world," so neither Islam nor Orthodox Christianity nor Buddhism died in the Buryat Republic during that seventy years of "Babylonian captivity" of Communist rule any more than Judaism died as a result of the Holocaust.

When the Soviet Union did fall, I was shocked. I had gone there to see Communism in action. From what I saw, Communism was a force that we Americans—with our notion of liberty and openness to other ideas, our belief that we had achieved a better approximation of truth—would just have to contend with for a long time to come.

How wrong I was!

For which I am so glad.

Those four days "with the people" should have indicated to me, though at the time to my consciousness it did not, that "the people" have some kind of inner push toward greater knowledge and truth. In the words of William Cullen Bryant, often quoted by Martin Luther King, "Truth crushed to earth shall rise again." Some would call that "inner push" spirit or soul, but I am content to leave it as "human inner push."

Even after using one thousand "failed words" to describe that four days on the Tashkent Express, I am still sure that I have not begun to convey the tremendous impact this train journey had on me.

కావ

Another quite memorable train ride was from La Paz across the Andes down to the coast at Arica, Chile. Unlike the others, on this train I was *sick*. It may have been altitude sickness, but I think not.

This train's third class had very hard seats if a seat was even available. I did get to sit for the entire trip—in two sections—probably because someone deferred to me. We were very crowded just as buses in South America always were. Sickeningly so! Also like buses, the railroad followed a very winding route. At several points out the window, I could see the engine or caboose (or even both?) in a sharp-turning curve around the mountains.

The constant swaying of the train was enough to make me suffer motion sickness I had never felt before or since.

Food? Last thing I wanted! I think the kindly Aymara, Quechua, and other indigenous people on the train did offer from their stores, but I could not have eaten even if I felt hungry. Most of them, too, showed signs of discomfort, though not as acute as mine. I saw most of them coped by chewing coca leaves from their little belt pouches to get into a semi-comatose state to endure the ride. I knew, too grievously, that they also engaged in this habit to endure their harsh lives of eternal poverty and cold in the Altiplano.

The Altiplano was always cold. So, too, was this train. I would have expected such a mass of closely packed bodies would generate more heat.

The kindly natives saw that I was suffering even more than they were and offered me their only surcease—their coca leaves to chew. Coca is raw cocaine. Even amid my misery I was not tempted, but appreciated their kindness in the offering to help me bear the misery.

To make matters worse, as in many other countries I had visited except the United States/Canada border and on the Orient Express, the transport did not cross the frontier. I had to disembark and walk over or take another train or bus to the second country.

This Bolivian train stopped at the *cumbre* (summit). The Andes divide being so very high in altitude, *bitter* cold is the rule there. Normally the Chilean train or bus is waiting, so crossing is usually a brief matter after the two border formalities.

Not this time. We were delayed at nearly the top of the world for what seemed *hours* in the bitterest cold I have ever felt. Why did I not dig out the sleeping bag for warmth, as I had to cross Paso del condor? I'll never know. I must have kept expecting that the connecting train would arrive any minute.

Some enterprising small group built a fire for warmth but that barely cut the cold. I do not know what they used for fuel. It was the most miserable wait that I ever experienced, for there was no station, nothing at all for shelter.

I do not even recall a building for the customs and passport control officials. Looking back, I wonder whether there was a jeep trail down; maybe they had gone? More likely, the formalities were exchanged inside the two trains making buildings necessary.

Eventually the Chilean train did come, but I did not warm up clear to Arica.

కాల్క

Unwilling to repeat the misery of crossing the Andes third class, when I was ready to continue into Argentina, I went first class.

I have never heard about any "second" class; why the gap? Actually, they do not refer to third class either, only "hard seats." On that day, I did not see what conditions were like in the hard seats, but in the first-class section, with its upholstery, there were *many* empty seats.

This was a night crossing. I must have slept through most of the crossing because I do not remember the twisting and steepness as before. At the *cumbre* frontier post, we stepped out of the Chilean train immediately onto the Argentine train, so I never got chilled. Then I must have slept again, for I recall nothing of the journey until the next morning on the plains of Argentina.

By my choosing a night train over a day schedule, let no one think I had a choice among several trains each day. As I recall, the trains only ran two or three times a week. Of course I could have more scheduling flexibility had I taken a plane, but that is my least favorite mode of transportation.

As I got off the train in the town of Jujuy (pronounced Hoohooey), Argentina, I smelled a delightful scent—the sweet smell blossoms from many orange trees. Later I was among the orange groves around Lake Wales, Florida. I cannot explain the difference and though the aroma there was delightful, it was not nearly as so wonderful as that I experienced in Jujuy!

కాల్క

I discovered some images from Rudyard Kipling's poem, "Mandalay," which made me feel ignorant not to have recognized before I was there to see and hear them for myself. For example, that road to Mandalay is not a road on land, which I should have known from the fact that flying fish do not play on a terrestrial route, but the sea lane by ship across the Bay of Bengal. I did manage to spy a few flying fish playing there from the ship I took from Calcutta, India, to Chittagong in Bangladesh, to Yongon, the capital of Myanmar.

Loving ships, I did not mind the sea travel. I thrilled to see the dawn come up like thunder across the Bay from China—Indochina—which included Myanmar and more of Southeast Asia or China in Kipling's day when he wrote the poem. As for his image of dawn coming up like thunder, I had already experienced "thunderous" sunrises in Puerto Rico and later in India. The term refers to the great rapidity of light-to-dark and dark-to-light in the tropics. One moment it is full daylight when the sun appears just at the horizon. Only a moment or two later the sun appears to have dropped completely below the horizon and the world is pitch black. Amazing.

I had also seen the opposite phenomenon in the almost Arctic in Alaska where I lived for three years. The sun dropped below the horizon at approximately 11 p.m., but the night never appeared totally dark. In summer, we had *long* and very light twilight. If you stay up late enough, and I did stay up all "night" once simply to check it out, this was not the twilight of a setting sun but the dawn of rising sun.

Still a long, long time passes before the sun rises above the horizon. In winter the phenomenon was not as pronounced, but somehow at sunset, around 3 p.m., the sky, though full of stars, was a dark yet light bright blue of indescribable beauty. We never experienced true darkness then either, even without a moon's light. What amazed me was that before my trip, I did not grasp from Kipling's words what he meant. I had to experience it for myself.

I also discovered that Kipling's "temple-bells" of the "old Moulmein pagoda" are not bells but *chimes*: very thin, light, metal "leaves" to represent the leaves of the bodhi tree under which Buddha, the Enlightened One, found his enlightenment. These chimes are positioned around one of the upper tiers of the pagoda so that each can catch the breeze. As hot as it was when I was there, and being a tropical climate most likely year-round, there nearly always seemed some slight breeze to play the chimes and please the people. The light musical tinkle of similar pagoda "bells" can be heard all over Myanmar. But despite its Buddhist tradition, I never noticed such bells in Thailand or other Buddhist places.

On the big boats heading down the Irrawaddy River from Moulmein, people would spread mats for sleeping and use the same mats for seating during the day. I used my sleeping bag for this purpose. There on deck passengers cooked their morning and afternoon rice over small camp stoves. It never failed that some smiling woman of a family group would bring me a plate of rice, too! I lived very well on those Burmese riverboats!

But on this fluvial network the boat was too small for even these limited sleeping and cooking practices. I did not know how things would go but felt confident that the local people had sleeping and cooking arrangements well practiced. As had been my habit abroad and sometimes in the United States, I would watch and do as they did.

Meanwhile the jungle around us seemed to glide by the boat. Mental effort was required to realize that this was an illusion—the boat was gliding. I have experienced that same sensation on long bus rides. The vast land of the

United States appears to roll past the window and I have to make a mental adjustment keep in mind that the moving object is the bus window.

Even though I had learned that Rudyard Kipling's "Road to Mandalay" evoked the sea lane by ship across the Bay of Bengal, on that Irrawaddy riverboat, I thought instead it might mean this river road instead.

The river boat pulled over at a bank that had a wooden platform covered by a thatched roof. As soon as the boat docked, people scrambled out and put their mats down on the floor in the orderly rows just as they had done on the deck of the Irrawaddy steamer. I followed their pattern.

Now I usually carried an emergency supply of non-perishable food, but in Myanmar I never needed to. As soon as passengers boarded and settled themselves, they began preparing their afternoon rice. It was their belief and custom that they gained merit for sharing with a stranger in their midst. They did not view their acts as charity. We repeated the same process for morning rice before we boarded the boat tied there overnight.

Did I spend just the one night on that fluvial network, or more? The memory of my experience is so vivid that it seems as if I must have spent two or even three nights in those free platform shelters in the jungle next to the riverbank with people gaining merit by feeding me morning and afternoon rice each day. I forget the detail of what we did about sanitary facilities but there must have been something because Burmese people are fastidiously clean. We finally came to the end of that segment of river travel at the little port town of Mergui.

What impressed me most here was the orderliness by which these Burmese Buddhist people lined themselves up on deck for everyone's greater good and the kindliness by which they fed me morning and afternoon rice. Kindliness may not be the right word, as there is a completely different attitude toward such in many Oriental cultures.

"Begging" is not the right word for the bowls Buddhist monks carry at dawn. Instead of begging because they need or desire to obtain food, these monks are giving people the opportunity to accumulate merit for the next life. The Buddhists' smiling offer of rice and my smiling acceptance was part of that merit system. They were adding merit for their next life and I was helping them to do that. I think that the monks accepting the gifts did not add demerit for the next life: they, too, obtaining merits for giving the gift of opportunity to obtain merits to the rice givers.

I never figured out exactly how this system differs from Christian charity, but it does, and both systems differ from *Zakat* (loosely translated, alms or charity) in the Muslim world, which are obligatorily paid alms to support social services out of a sense of justice, not charity, because it is right for the wealthy to share in the All-Beneficent One's riches with the less fortunate.

Judaic tradition appears to have a better grasp of this distinction between justice and charity than the Christian tradition that confuses the two.

Jews distinguish between self-perceived non-obligatory kindness of a giver as opposed to self-perceived obligation or duty of a person to pay back an accumulated debt.

Thus I observed similar attitudes relative to charity or alms giving in three or four major religions. I was not sure about the Hindu belief in this regard, but since Hindus believe in reincarnation until they reach Nirvana, perhaps this concept of merit accumulation might be found in their tradition also.

&∽✍

Later I took a steamboat on the Nile from Aswan, Egypt, to Wadi Halfa on the Sudan border. What a *difference*!

On the Irrawaddy, deck passengers rode on the open deck on their reed mats for both sitting during the day and for sleeping at night. I was quite surprised to see how much a reed mat softened the hardness of the wooden deck, making the seat quite comfortable, much more so than a semi-featherbed or sleeping bag.

On the Nile boat on the other hand, third-class passengers were below deck in steerage. There were two of these holds for the human cargo: one for men and one for women and children. But the biggest difference was that instead of lining themselves in orderly rows as the Burmese had, people put down their bedding to claim their own spacing in helter-skelter fashion. This made the situation unbearable to me. In that stinking hold, I could not see a thing of the scenery we steamed by, which after seeking answers was a big, if not the chief, attraction of travel.

I sought out the purser to change my passage to first class, which had cabins. But the cabins were all full.

What to do? I took my sleeping bag up and spread it on deck. As on any large ship, people were on deck in deck chairs or just on mats as at a beach. At night in hot weather, passengers took bedding out of their cabins to spend the night on deck. Thus I was not alone and not conspicuous. No passenger or boat officer gave me a second glance during the whole journey, so it was very comfortable and rewarding.

As for food, since I had not paid for first-class passage, I thought eating in the first-class dining room would not be fair and might be embarrassing. The word for the "cheap hold" was to carry food that required no cooking and I had brought along my own. I never thought of my self-help as "stealing service," for I had *offered* to pay.

There was a sidebar to this journey.

In the crowd on the dock at Aswan before boarding, I met a young American man also traveling steerage. We exchanged a few remarks. Later in the gender-segregated holds, we never saw one another again until disembarking at Wadi Halfa. He reported that being in the "hell hole" was all that he could possibly endure. He wondered how I had managed. I replied that I had not suffered or dealt with mere endurance; I had enjoyed positive luxury by moving up on deck. He was astonished. Moving had never occurred to him.

I do not know whether he ever tried incurring the additional cost to get first-class passage. If he had, he may have met with the same obstacle that I did. We were soon separated in the press of boarding the train for Khartoum, Sudan—passengers did not line up but all tried to crowd in all at once—and I never saw him again.

కొం

After steaming down the Irrawaddy and up the Nile, the huge riverine road left as *the* road, where there is no land road, is the mighty Amazon River in South America.

I had gotten from Rondonopolis to Puerto Velho, Brazil, riding with the oil barrels aboard a truck on those "not quite" roads. From Puerto Velho, I boarded a steamer down the Rio Madeira to the confluence of the Amazon not far from Manaus, Brazil. The Ohio and Missouri Rivers are big, but the Rio Madeira is as large as both of them put together. The Andes makes bigger headwaters than the Rocky Mountains, I gathered.

I was told the price included meals so did not take my own food. I became uneasy at seeing other passengers carrying a lot of food. I found out why with the first meal, which was exactly the same as all others: a tin plate of the worst excuse for stew I ever ate. Breakfast was more edible, coffee and a hunk of bread.

Luckily, we were confined to the hold only at night, being allowed out on deck during the day. I again attempted to pay extra to obtain first-class passage, but again there was none to be had. This time I could not sleep on deck. In addition to the horrific odor in the hold, passengers hung hammocks every which way. This arrangement might appear to leave plenty of room on the floor beneath the hammocks, except that parents carried infants and children with them above. After the first accident, I tried to place myself where no children were around. That went reasonably well.

Having learned that there would be no first-class passage available after the stopover in Manaus, I intended to get some food for the rest of the trip. But I had another priority in Manaus and needed to return to the steamer before obtaining any food. This trip was the time I recall in all of my travels abroad where I had what I considered a food problem. Why?

Corruption is a way of life in much of the world but I think *the* worst in Brazil. The company that operated the steamer might have operated the food service that way for greater profiteering. Or possibly the company did not know and the food service provided the corruption, pocketing *cruzeiros* that were supposed to be spent for better food.

I have no idea what the first-class food was like. One sure thing, the meals on the truck journey across the Mato Grosso were far and away better than the meals aboard that steamer. I wondered, too, at the probability of classism: The truck driver negotiated face to face and was in a power position. Whereas people too poor to go except by steerage may not be considered to have sufficient value to rate decent conditions and are powerless to protest or to choose any better.

Is it odd that "free" choice so often is not free at all? How often must we pay, often pay a lot, to choose desirable alternatives?

I am perfectly free to choose between one-hundred-dollar jeans and twenty-dollar jeans. But if I do not have one hundred dollars, how free am I to choose?

Even with plenty of money and the willingness to spend it, if first-class passage is already sold out and my visa is about to expire, as mine was, then how free am I?

Of course I was always quite free never to go abroad in the first place, free not to have traveled there at all. I could have gone with a group that chartered only first-class passage all the way in advance. I had nearly unlimited other options along the way that impacted on the choices left to me then.

I made my choices and every single time found whatever it was *well* worth the price I paid, nearly always far above, far better than I had ever supposed it would be.

⁖

Despite having to endure uncomfortable conditions on the steamer down the Rio Madeira and then down the Amazon from Manaus to Belem, Brazil, just being on this widest river of our whole planet was thrilling for me. I read later of some natural history tours of the Amazon, which described the wonderful exotic sights to be seen along the shores. I could only conclude that that tour boat purposely stayed close to shore so that tourists could see those sights.

The boat I took must have more pedestrian purposes catering to business travelers or others not so interested in sightseeing. These people may not have had a burning desire to see the sights as they lived amid them daily. Whatever the reason, our boat navigated the midstream and the river is so wide that I could barely make out the shore on either side in the dim distance.

But that, too, is a big part of the awe of steaming down the Amazon, an awesome experience indeed, far and beyond paltry considerations as harsh conditions of the boat. After all, I had nearly a whole lifetime ahead for the comfort of my own home and all the great meals I wanted because I was fortunate enough to always have been able to find a job that would enable me to afford a comfortable home and plenty of good food. For travel abroad I had always been content to travel third class.

I found many words to describe some negative aspects of the steamboat that carried me on the Amazon and now find that I have used far fewer words to describe the glory of that riverine road upon which the steamboat carried me. Even so—the experience was truly a glory to me.

&~&

From the first moment, I began walking up the gangway of the *S.S. United States* in January 1956 for my first travel abroad I fell in love with sea lanes and ships, waterways and boats as the best way to travel. Even though the world has changed so much that sailing has become nearly extinct, I have never changed my mind.

So after stretching a budget originally planned for a three-month stay in Europe into ten months instead, my finances were running out. In addition, I wanted to return home by Election Day. So I went to the harbor master in Haifa, Israel, to inquire about passage to the United States. There was no ship immediately available, but a Jewish refugee ship was due shortly full of North African orphans. That ship would take on passengers headed for Europe and then pick up another load of Jewish immigrants bound for return to Israel.

While the port of arrival in Europe was not yet confirmed, surely there would be passage to the United States available from that port. So I secured passage on this ship. That must have been a Friday because I saw the strangest thing, to me, just after Sabbath, Saturday sunset.

The ship steamed into port and the gangplank lowered. The passengers came off, hundreds of children, each carrying a suitcase or small satchel. Social workers were there to meet the children and guide them to buses that would carry them to a *kibbutz* or wherever. These buses, too, had obviously been prepared on Friday to wait over Sabbath. I was amazed there could have been so many Jewish orphans in North Africa. But there they were now in their Promised Land—Israel.

I boarded as soon as the last child left the ship. Because this was not a regular passenger ship, it only took "chance passengers." Only a handful of other passengers joined me. Some were European Jews who, in their enthusiasm for Israel, had gone to live in *kibbutzim* but became disillusioned and were returning to Europe. Somehow, in social innovations we do not hear much about disillusionment, but I suppose it always happens.

The big topic of conversation en route was where we would land. Despite hoping that we would land in Marseilles, France, we were not disappointed that we landed in Genoa, Italy, instead.

In Genoa I went to the harbor master to inquire about ships going to the United States, preferably a freighter, in the near future. A freighter, the *Federico Costa* would arrive at any time and leave for the United States in a few days. Depending on the cargo, the ship would put ashore along the East Coast of the United States, certainly at Philadelphia and New York.

There was a big load of lumber on deck, so I sat on the lumber mostly in great comfort, just being one with the circle of the ocean. I find several consecutive days of travel on ships especially, but also trains and buses, to be blissfully idyllic, restful interludes during which ordinary life demands and frustrations are suspended for the duration of the voyage or trip.

On the *S.S. United States* it was a time to dream of the great new experiences Europe would bring me. On the *Federico Costa*, it was time to relive those experiences. Oh, yes, I had some frightening encounters, but overall I found to my glad surprise that the reality had been much better than I had ever dreamed it would be. I rated my trip as a great success even though I had not found what I was looking for—solutions to human social problems.

Did I conclude there are no real solutions? For each alternative considered, I could think of some possible drawback. Could we only collectively keep on trying to alleviate some small problem as we can or as we are willing? I do not think that I came to any particular conclusion, but I *enjoyed* being there on top of the lumber pile with circle of sea and sky around me with no problems to solve—until the voyage ended—but I did not think of that as the ship plowed steadily on.

The first port of call was Newport News, Virginia. I would have loved to remain aboard all the way to New York, but that would have cost quite a bit more money and time, both of which were running out for me, so Newport News it would have to be.

ॐ

The bus station at Newport News, Virginia, was some two or three miles from the dock. I opted for foot travel, as I like that, too, when I have the time. We landed on a Sunday. The sidewalk from dock to city center lay through the then "colored," now "Afro-American," part of town. This area was not a slum at all but a neat, residential section of well-painted houses and well-mowed lawns, some being mowed just as I passed because weekday jobs require homeowners to do household chores during leisure time on weekends.

As expected on a Sunday, some backyard barbecues were slightly visible from the front. Some parents were enjoying a Sunday walk with their children in strollers. This was the sort of scene I expected in middle-class white America, but these were black families! I thought many of them must be workers at the big naval base, so the area was not poverty-stricken.

I marveled at the children's eyes, which I had never consciously noticed before: They were shiny, bright, and healthy looking. I began to question my picture of "oppressed minority victims" of "shameful racism!"

I knew then beyond a doubt, and have not found contrary evidence since, that in spite of our appalling, shameful, sociopolitical evils in the United States, this country still offers the best opportunity for more abundant life to the most people than any other nation I explored in my travels.

We need desperately to correct some of the most glaring and grievous evils, but sometimes I see some signs of hope that maybe we are progressing. Unfortunately, we also tend to regress some, too, at times. We can only keep trying.

ॐॐ

In 1967, I took freighter passage from La Guaira, the port for Caracas, Venezuela, across the Gulf of Mexico to New Orleans, Louisiana. This time I knew this would be my last voyage, my last travel abroad, because my curiosity had been slaked. I landed in New Orleans with feelings of both relief and euphoria.

I had traveled on many roads on land, including railroads; on the waters of oceans, rivers, and lakes; and in the air. I had gone to and from many different countries and traveled all around our fifty United States. But though I looked for the best to be found in each of the other lands, I had not found better elsewhere.

STUDY QUESTIONS

1. In the introduction, the author states that the primary purpose of her travel was "Because I wanted to see how other countries ordered their institutions to achieve the best possible life for its citizens."
   - Is the extensive focus on roads and the places connected by the roads consistent with this stated purpose?
   - In what way might the roads be metaphorical for how countries order their institutions? Support your position with examples from the chapter.

2. About the reason for crossing a rope bridge over a gorge at Machu Picchu, the author says, "What possessed me to cross that bridge? I do not know. Maybe it was for a 'fool Yankee' notion of thrill after all."
   - Does this statement sound like a self-realization of a value not previously recognized by the author or a reluctant admission for need of a reason in the face of apparently contradiction between her stated values and her actions?
   - What self-characterization might the author cherish that would make her reluctant to admit that she values thrill?

3. In the introduction, the author said, "I had a grandiose notion of returning from my travels with ideas about how to correct our faults as a nation."

- Did the author's experiences recounted in the roads chapter confirm or refute her preconceived notion that she would find life to be more abundant in countries other than the United States?
- Using evidence from this chapter, discuss values held by the author.

4. The author states that she began her travels looking for solutions because she believed that some Americans did not enjoy the same privileges as others in the United States. Then, describing a South American man critical of the United States, she says, "That man's image of the United States was so opposite to my naively optimist image of the country of my dream, with liberty and justice for all, our own people and others in the world. "

- Is this statement consistent with the claim that the author was dissatisfied with the United States or that she viewed the United States as a place where people were not enjoying equal access to the bounties in the United States?

5. The author asks, "Is it odd that 'free' choice so often is not free at all?"

- Discuss the cost of "free choice" in obtaining and securing values and other items of importance to you.

6. The author states that she was aware of "gross discrepancies between the incomes of CEOs by comparison to, say, janitors."

- Does this passage imply that the author viewed this as an example of the United States' economic system being unfair or repressive to the masses?
- Would the author would prefer to see CEOs and janitors earn the same amount for their work?
- Discuss reasons such a system would be fair or not fair.
- Does this author appear to favor socialism or capitalism? Support your position with examples from the text in this or other chapters.

Four

WAR!

I feel considerable diffidence characterizing my brief, tame experiences with war, which loom large in my memory, when millions of men and women have had so many direct, brutal, bloody encounters that not only remain in their memories but vestiges of which also remain as physical damage in their bodies. But to me at the time, my terror was real yet softened and balanced by other inspirational encounters on the same trips.

My first encounter with war was my 1956 trip to Israel. I arrived just before war broke out with the Arabs, involving the Suez Canal and thus Britain and France. I went along the Jordan River to every place that someone had theorized in print might have been the site of Jesus' baptism. I discarded every one for not speaking to my heart until I stumbled on one along the bank of the Jordan River on the Israeli side.

Syria was on the opposite bank along this stretch not far from Beth Shean, Scythopolis, about seventeen miles south of the Sea of Galilee at the junction of the Harod and Jordan Valleys. I had found the theorized location in some booklet. I figured the location to be on the river bank at a certain *moshav*. In *kibbutzim* the people live communally, children in a children's dormitory with parental visitation from their dormitories. Also a cooperative, in the *moshav* families live together in houses much the same as other farm communities the world over.

I looked up the manager of the *moshav* and showed him the item I had found about the site of Jesus' baptism. He agreed that the site must be at this *moshav*, but to his knowledge no pilgrims before me had come there asking to cross to reach the river bank site. He was willing to allow me to cross but not alone. He detailed a young man to go with me. I was not too pleased at this provision, for sometimes I might have some kind of inspiration wherein such a site might "speak to my heart." I was pretty sure such could not be the case with a rifle-carrying stranger waiting beside me.

Being armed with rifles was not unusual for the tractors of *kibbutzim* and *moshavim*. Threat of wild animals existed as well as the threat of Arabs. To see the site at all, I had to agree.

Admittedly, I really wanted to see the Jordan from a different vantage point more than I thought this would be the site of Jesus' baptism because there was no evidence that I knew of supporting the writer's claim. More credible "evidence" indicates that it would be more logical to conclude that the place would more likely be located near the Jericho Ford, where there might naturally be more people to whom the forerunner could preach.

With my escort I went through a cornfield to the river bank. No good way to get down the bank to the water, or any place for a crowd to gather, was there. Though I had no way to know how the scene might have been two millennia earlier, I could not fathom this as the site.

So there I was at this *moshav*, looking at the Jordan, when suddenly from the corner of my eye I spied a glint. I reacted with reflex action: I hit the sandy dirt. Going down in the flood of adrenalin, I still had presence of mind to think that I would explain to the Israeli guide that I thought I had seen the glint of a rifle barrel across the Jordan in Syria. No need for explanation though, for he was right in the sandy dirt beside me.

We lay there for quite a little while until he crawled a bit downstream away from me and very cautiously peeped over the tall grass on the bank. After a while thus, he got up and motioned to me. We quietly made our way back away from where sentries were patrolling the river frontier.

I defy anyone to have any sort of inspirational experience with guns of war so close by. I surely had no inspirational encounter at that site.

⇛⇘

My second encounter with war fortunately had a humorous ending. In 1962, I landed in Tangier, Morocco, with a plan to go almost across the entire Sahara Desert, to Egypt, then down the Nile south to Sudan and across to Addis Ababa, Ethiopia, and beyond in a seven months or so African odyssey. I say almost across the Sahara because the Mediterranean rim with road and railroad is not the Sahara proper, which would be too tough for me and I supposed not that rewarding.

For several years, Algeria had engaged in guerilla warfare against France fighting for its independence. France was finally about to grant Algerian independence shortly. But I never supposed guerilla warfare would affect me since they had called a truce while independence negotiations ensued.

Tangier and its Casbah were fascinating, but I did not care for the dish couscous, made from ground barley I think, or mint tea. I tried to get tea without mint, but making tea without mint is just not done in Morocco.

While in Tangier, I took the ferry over to Gibraltar and Spain to see the superb Alhambra at Granada. I have regretted ever since that I did not take the extra time to go on to Madrid and El Prado, Spain, but I was in a hurry to get back to Tangier in order to cross the frontier into Algeria. We all make mistakes in life.

Having learned from my trips to Turkey and the Soviet Union that sometimes the frontier-crossing formalities must be done in the capital or some other sizeable city far from the actual frontier, I started the process in Tangier—and hit a snag.

The French official there refused to grant me a visa to enter Algeria. I was trying to think of my next move when another minor official motioned to me. This one told me that amid the delicate negotiations going on between France and Algeria, the French were backing off from what would become Algerian affairs in just days. They were no longer granting visas. He suggested that if I went to the Algerian provisional government there in Tangier they might give me the documentation to enter.

The Algerian provisional government headquarters was inconspicuous amid the alleys of Tangier but I found it and explained why I was there. The official was sympathetic but explained that Algeria still did not have the right to issue visas. Amid the delicate negotiations going on, Algeria did not want to do anything to offend the French. Alternatively, he said that I might just board the train at the frontier without a visa and if challenged, "show 'this.'"

"This" was a tiny wooden star and crescent, symbol of Islam throughout the Muslim world. I am still puzzled about the power of the little token he gave to me, for I thought anyone could buy the same in any bazaar or *souk* for a few cents. I was challenged three or four times in Algeria, but on seeing the tiny emblem, was allowed to pass.

First I had to get on the train to Algiers at the frontier. Moroccan exit formalities were nothing but on the Algerian side, a young Frenchman met us. First, he noted that I had no visa for Algeria, so I showed the token. He shook his head, which I understood perfectly: This might be an open-sesame pass for Algerians but it meant nothing to France. He scratched his head at the problem, then asked to be excused for the rest room. I wondered if, by his action, he was signaling me that he did not dare openly let me through but that I should just go on to the train. I did not wait to wonder for long—just went.

Normally a passenger must show authorization papers in order to purchase a ticket. I do not now recall that detail, but there was not even a pause. Neither do I recall the detail of changing Moroccan money to Algerian money, but later it haunted me that I had no Algerian money, only U.S. travelers checks. It may be they took that as currency for the ticket with whatever Moroccan money needed to make up the difference.

I meant to keep that little wooden star and crescent as a souvenir but soon lost it.

಄ఴ

Occasionally a conductor looked at my ticket but always returned it. He must have punched it. What made the trip foreboding were the frequent, chilling signs of war in every town: barbed wire barricading everywhere, machine guns on roofs of banks and schools. On banks was understandable, to thwart guerilla robberies to finance operations. But schools? At least I thought these buildings had to be schools, but perhaps not. Nonetheless, inside the train I felt safe and was safe, as long as I was inside the train.

The thought never occurred to me that guerillas might blow up the tracks, causing a wreck that would injure or kill passengers and crew. Fortunately, no such incident occurred.

As we came to a station in the city of Oran, Algeria, passengers began to disembark. I soon realized in puzzlement that everyone was getting off. As was my habit in such situations, I followed their lead and got off too, or maybe by then a conductor motioned me out.

By then darkness had fallen, a darkness more black than I had ever experienced. Only later did I learn the reason for how dark it was.

I had no idea when the train would load up again. No one seemed to be waiting for that; they had gone away somewhere. There may have been one last employee in the dark who let me know that the train would not continue until morning, or I may have decided that had to be the case. In resignation I headed for a hotel until the next day. Having no Algerian currency, or not enough to pay for the hotel, I got out two or three travelers checks and started to hunt for a hotel that I knew would typically be located near the station.

Even in the pitch black darkness I found a building that, though dark on the outside, had murmurs coming from inside that suggested I had found a hotel and that it was still open. The door was locked, but I had learned from previous travel in the boondocks that they would accept customers even after they had already gone to bed. The accepted procedure was to pound on the door until someone was roused. (Hostels, on the other hand, had strict curfews. At those places, the normal procedure in similar circumstances was to sack out on the doorstep and sleep until morning.)

When someone came to the door, I showed the fistful of U.S. travelers checks, but he slammed the door in my face.

I was dismayed but not alarmed.

Undaunted, I made for a second hotel. That door was also locked.

I went through the pounding again until someone finally opened it. I thrust my traveler checks out to indicate I wanted a bed, but again the person slammed the door in my face.

Returning to the station to sack out until morning would do no good, as the last man out with me had locked the door behind us. What to do? I wanted to stay near the station to avoid getting lost in the black darkness.

The only solution that came to me was to sack out someplace until morning, which I did, practically on the sidewalk. Homeless in Oran, with plenty of money yet in a belt under my clothing!

Still I was not alarmed. No one seemed to be stirring about who would bother me. I did not picture Algerians as cutthroats as I might have feared in American big cities. In moments I was asleep.

Shortly I woke with a feeling of sudden alarm and terror. Two soldiers were poking through my sleeping bag with rifles!

Perhaps if I kept still they would go away, I thought, or so I hoped. What else *could* I do against soldiers with rifles? I could not understand what they were saying at all but thought that one was French and the other Algerian, evidently some effort at bipartisan patrolling on these very few days last before Algerian independence when the French would turn over all such matters to the Algerians.

Apparently they did not decide that I was harmless. They did not just go away. I guessed that my sleeping bag caught their attention since locals would only wrap some sort of shawl around them.

As natural in the throes of anxiety, my imagination pictured me pulled out, robbed, raped, and shot in the streets of Oran. Even now, I cannot fathom why I felt more terrified in the presence of soldiers than with civilian men. It did not occur to me then, but now as I recount the tale I think that they could have been brigands, not soldiers, out for anything they could get. Rifles were common among the guerillas as well as among soldiers.

The pairing of Algerian and French is, I think, what made me conclude that these two were soldiers. The French, I knew, had more Algerians in their forces than French, as British in India had more Indians than Brits, and similarly in other places in the dominion if my recollection is accurate.

At any rate, my keeping-still strategy was not working, so I decided on another measure. Maybe if I screamed out in English, they might recognize me as English or American and believe molesting a Brit or American would be worse than accosting one of their citizens because they might incur terrible consequences. I screamed out as loud as I could in English, "Get away and leave me alone!"

Their reply I understood perfectly: One of them—I could not tell whether the French or Algerian—gasped, "My God, a German woman!" and they *ran*.

Thank goodness! Who would have thought German women to be so tough that they cow French and Algerian soldiers! I have wondered ever since just how either came to that impression. I had no time to wonder about that then though, because although I do not recall falling asleep, my next conscious awareness was morning, my night of terror was over.

ॐॐ

I am so naive about war in actual experience by contrast to many, many people of my generation that I still did not consider my encounter with the soldiers on the street of Oran as one of war. That did not come until a day or two later.

First, I returned to the railroad station, which by the time I awakened was already open. After a long while the train left for Algiers, Algeria's largest city and the end of the line for this train. Arriving in Algiers during daylight, gaining entrance to a hotel presented no problem. I think that the hotel must have changed money. There being barbed wire barricading and machine guns on roof tops, I would remember having done business in a bank that day.

Although my speaking fluency in French was insufficient to carry on conversation easily, I was able to read French fairly well. A newspaper that I picked up had an account of the biggest battle of the Algerian War to date in Oran, the night before last, when I had slept outdoors in the same town and never even suspected! Only after reading the account of battle did I realize that the black night had been the blackout of war.

Amid all the shooting, I had slept through? Yes. I have always been a very sound sleeper. To wake me took rifles poking me in my sleeping bag and even after the fright I had fallen fast asleep nearly immediately.

When I thought of big battles of war, the World War II Battle of the Bulge came to mind, with so many thousands and thousands fighting amid canons and heavy artillery. The actuality of such horror is beyond my comprehension.

But this Algerian War for Independence was mainly guerilla warfare fought on a much smaller scale. Despite the truce during the final negotiations, with the agreement to restore independence to Algeria already decided, someone had broken the truce. I do not remember which side initiated the hostility. Thirty people were reported killed, with many more wounded. The difference in scale between this "biggest battle of the Algerian War to date" and other "big" battles was remarkable to me.

The paper was full of assurances from both sides that even though the apparent intent of the attack was to break off negotiations, these would continue and independence would come for Algeria as scheduled. I think both sides claimed that the instigators had been hothead extremists not connected with the official leaders of either side.

The next day or the following day, I witnessed the official end of the Algerian War for Independence in the independence ceremony. My hotel had a balcony with a fine view of the ceremonies in the square where the French Tricolor flew.

At dawn trucks filled with men and women streamed into Algiers. To me there seemed to be more women than men. They hopped off the trucks and stood around in the square. Soon the square was packed. Nearly all wore traditional Algerian dress: white ankle-length bloomer pantaloons, knee-length green tunic above, and either white or green headscarf. I did not notice anyone wearing *burqas* or *chadors*, or face masks that Muslim women often wore as an alternative to the full veil of *burqa*. A few men wore Western-style dress. I supposed they were French. I also supposed that some Algerian men might also be wearing Western-style clothing because they had adopted that fashion for ordinary occasions. The traditional styles being worn that day appeared to be celebratory and symbolic of their heritage.

I was surprised to see no French or Algerian military guards of honor except the barest handful for the actual hauling of the ropes later. At noon, the French flag was lowered and the green and white Star and Crescent was raised.

I was surprised by the emotionality of the people as the Tricolor was hauled down. The Algerians saw independence as the embodiment of great hope and high expectations for their future. For the French, Algerian independence marked the end of a grand world empire and greatly reduced power and influence for France.

I had been on the side of Algeria, as I am sympathetic with any "struggle for liberation" against a controlling power. I always hope that the controlling power will have the wisdom to see change as inevitable and give up without war.

The situation in Algeria was complicated by the length of time France had ruled there. Many French Algerians were third-, or fourth-generation citizens who, while still speaking French (probably with Arabic), no longer had any ties to France. Leaving Algeria meant giving up their homes, livelihoods, and lifestyle. As an era changes for the betterment of the majority, the changes always leave some minority faced with a darker future instead of a glad one.

I found myself standing near a blonde woman and her little five-, or six-year-old blonde son, whom I took to be French. Talking with children in Spanish or French is easier for me than speaking with adults in those languages, so I spoke to the child in fractured French, attempting to engage him in a bit of friendly teasing.

He drew himself up and said in French that was perfectly understandable to me, "I am not French but an Algerian man!"

The boy's mother then spoke to me in fluent English after recognizing my fractured French. She and her husband were among the French who had opted to take their chances and stay in the new Algeria. She acknowledged there would be problems, but they figured the future better for them and their son in this land that was now familiar to them than the land of their ancestors that they no longer knew personally.

So you see, I did not recognize that I had been at the scene of the biggest battle of the Algerian War for Independence until two days later. But the fright of waking to being prodded by rifle barrels stays with me all these years later.

STUDY QUESTIONS

1. The encounters with war in this chapter appear to indicate that the author traveled freely in several war zones, apparently without any fear for her own safety or anticipation that she might be in danger.

- What emotions did the author appear to experience in the face of what she describes as war situations?

- What values do the author's actions imply in these episodes?
- Do you think that the author displayed courage or recklessness?
- Would you have made different choices? Discuss your choices and reasons for making them.

2. Describing the independence ceremony in Algeria, the author states that she saw many women, but not many women wearing burqas or other veils.

- What do you think accounts for this observation?

3. The author describes experiencing terror when two men poked rifles into her sleeping bag as she slept on the street in Oran, Algeria. Then she says that she fell fast asleep immediately after they ran away from her.

- Do you think that the author's ability to fall asleep indicates that her claim to have been terrified was exaggerated?
- Given the same circumstances as described, how would you have handled the situation when you found yourself without a hotel that night?
- Is the author's description of this scenario believable?

Five

IN THE MUSLIM WORLD

What I am calling "the Muslim world" here is how I thought what I saw in some countries reflected on the religion of Islam and how these cultures were influenced by Islamic religion.

In the United States marriage is monogamous by law in every state. Monogamy was also the custom in most places before it was law, I think. In some places such as the Utah territory before Utah became a state though, religious custom allowed, even commanded, polygamy. The difference between custom and law was easier to distinguish in those communities. As I traveled in the Muslim world, sharp distinctions between religious custom and law were not as obvious. For Islam is a complete culture, not just a religion. It colors and shapes every aspect of life.

In1960, I saw evidence of Muslim heritage such as mosques in the central Asian republics of Kazakhstan, Uzbekistan, and Tajikistan, but no other evidence of people openly practicing Islam. Granted, in those countries, the way Intourist was set up at that time, a tourist had to be clever or lucky to meet people in natural settings that would illustrate their way of life.

I think by law the Soviets had prohibited visible displays of religious affiliation such as the *chador* veil for women, gender segregation in the schools, and other practices common to Islamic custom. Even if the Muslim religion thrived, the casual visitor would not have noticed; I did not personally perceive those countries as Muslim when I was there.

Since the break up of the Soviet Union, I understand that there has been a resurgence of Islam and the Russian Orthodox religion as well as open practice of custom, though I suppose they might not return to some older practices such as polygamous marriage or gender segregation in the schools. In other countries, I saw Islamic tradition openly practiced among a majority of people.

In Istanbul mosques struck me as far superior to Christian churches for serenity. A salient feature is that visitors must remove their shoes. I always have comfortable walking shoes but indoors I am much more at ease in bare feet. In the mosque, I sat on the floor with my back against the wall, more comfortable to me than sitting in a chair.

The decorative patterning in mosques, of geometric designs or stem-like intertwining also appealed to me. Stained glass requires no special looking. The mosque décor patterns were intricate and subtle; I found them more soothing than even the many Protestant churches I have visited that keep tenets of simplicity in mind in their design. Of course, my eyes and mind just skipped over the Qu'ranic verses found in mosques, since I do not read Arabic.

&-&

It was in Turkey that I observed an remarkable Islamic practice. The bus rolling along the highway across the steppe would occasionally pull off to the side and stop. Women stayed aboard with young children and daughters. Men filed out with sons from about age seven or eight to spread mats in rows. No explaining was necessary to know that they faced toward Mecca.

After the prayer pause, they re-boarded the bus, though not all together. Nor did I hear recitation. I thought each must have prayed at his own rate. At the time, I wondered whether this practice meant that Islamic women do not pray. A few years later in Pakistan I found that is not the case.

In Pakistan in 1960, where women wore black *burqa*s, I visited a girls' school, situated in a walled courtyard with classrooms on three sides of it. A molding around the wall had a row of pegs on which the little girls hung their *burqa*s after entering the courtyard.

Five times per day they all unrolled little mats, spread them on the floor, and prostrated themselves in the prescribed prayers of Islam.

I was told that the observance of prayer found in the religious schools might not be followed as strictly by the schoolchildren's parents at home. I think this is often the case that schoolchildren's observance might be demanded to be more strict by the school or parents in the interests of molding character and to instill values during the impressionable years.

&-&

Muslim dress and mosque architecture vary from country to country. Back in Turkey, Mustafa Kemal Atatürk outlawed outward shows of religion including "the veil" for women in 1923 when Turkey became a republic. At the same time, he established Turkey as a secular state where freedom of religion and women won suffrage. As a result, I never saw a veiled woman in Istanbul during my 1956 visit.

So I was surprised by a glimpse of Turkish-Muslim life out in some hinterlands. Women appeared to observe Atatürk's decree in the cities. In the rural agricultural areas, however, I saw women working in the fields wearing masks across the face below the eyes, different from the *hijab*, which is worn over the head, crossed at the throat, with the two ends hanging down the back. The secular reforms, it seemed, had not quite caught on yet in rural Turkey.

In one small Turkish town, I was able to meet a woman who did wear the *hijab*. She offered to introduce me to some of her friends at her home. The apartment was at the top of a flight of stairs. Six or eight young women arrived together carrying embroidery, but little stitching got done as we talked. They giggled a lot and talked among them, because only the hostess could field their questions, with difficulty. I suppose we may have suffered more misunderstanding than understanding.

At a point I noticed an abrupt change in mood among the women. They became quiet and to my surprise, each took out from some hidden place a facemask that they donned as they industriously began to embroider.

After a moment, I guessed that they were reacting to the sound of footsteps on the stairs. The hostess's husband had returned home. She explained my presence. The man was hospitable and welcoming. I was uneasy nonetheless, being unsure how to handle this situation, no longer an afternoon women's gossip gathering. The other guests appeared to react to the change as well and I followed their lead to leave shortly. I was intrigued to see how differently the women acted in the presence of a man not their husband.

Neither the Qu'ran, believed by Muslims to be the word of God revealed to Mohammed, nor the Hadith, a narration about the life of the Prophet, specifies any particular type of veil for women, but the Islamic teachings do advise "modesty" for both men and women. What constitutes "modesty" becomes a matter of cultural tradition or customary practice.

Arab tradition for men has included long robes and a *kuffiyeh* head covering as protection from blowing desert sands and that outfit covers as much, except for the face, as the women's garb. Perhaps the male beard is considered a symbolic face covering. But while the Qu'ran also enjoins modesty for men, they have never had extreme clothing imposed on them for that purpose. Unlike the women, who are prohibited from being seen in public without being covered in some Muslim countries, as practical needs have changed, men have been free to change their clothing styles at will. In my experience, in every culture, I have noticed that men adopt Western dress before the women do.

❧

In all my journeys, I tried to hear others' viewpoints about topics such as women's customary dress. In Peshawar, Pakistan, I borrowed a woman's *burqa* and wore it. She was the teacher of the girls' school class I had visited.

Peshawar had a big United States Air Force base at its edge and I think still does. The bookstore there had books in Urdu, the official language of Pakistan, and English.

On one occasion while I was wearing the *burqa* in the bookstore, two young American men from the airbase entered. They began talking in quite explicit sexual terms of what the young woman under the *burqa* must be like. They spoke as if they presumed that no one in the store could comprehend their conversation, spoken in English.

I was quite amused, but either by accident or design to cut off such talk, the proprietor asked me a direct question in English to which I felt obligated to respond. True, I had been in the store previously, but how he recognized me through the *burqa*, if he did, or realized that I was an American woman, I do not know. Perhaps he noticed my shoes.

When I answered, one soldier gasped, "My God—she's American!" The United States missed a great opportunity by not entering those two young men into the Olympics for sprinting. Not knowing if I would offend Pakistani sensibilities by laughing aloud, I could hardly wait to get out of the store to let loose my peals of laughter.

How does it feel to wear a *burqa*? In one, a feeling of anonymity or even invisibility descended on me. The eyeholes enabled me to see directly in front of me but cut off a significant portion of my range of vision. I do not know whether my perception was real or imaginary, but wearing the *burqa* seemed to cut down on hearing and smelling, too. Eating in a café was out of the question. For that I had to go back to my hotel room to take it off. That would not be such a problem to the women who lived there, as they would eat in the privacy of their homes where the *burqa* would not be worn. If male guests came into a home, it was custom for the women to stay in the kitchen unless serving the men when I suppose she might wear the *burqa*, but not while eating.

With the anonymity, I felt my world shrinking. I experienced a definite mental narrowing. But to describe this narrowing-down sensation in words is difficult. Even wearing the *burqa*, I could not imagine how I might feel had I never known wearing unrestrictive Western clothing before.

I think the purpose of such an all-concealing garment in the name of "modesty" is to prevent any male gaze of leering or lust or to prevent men from being distracted from worthwhile pursuits of study, work, or prayer. The five daily prayers and the Friday communal prayer involve prostration; a very immodest position in female garb somewhat mitigated by a *burqa*, but more mitigated by gender segregation in many activities and locations. That women might be distracted by men or that women's activities might require concentration and freedom from distraction never appeared to be considered.

ॐ

Another Muslim custom, *purdah* ("screen" or "veil"), is the practice that includes the seclusion of women from public observation by wearing concealing clothing from head to toe and by the use of high walls, curtains, and screens erected within the home. *Purdah* is practiced by Muslims and by various Hindus, especially in India and Pakistan. I did not personally observe *Purdah* when I was in Pakistan, but I did practice *purdah* in Libya when I spent three nights and two days with a man, his two wives, and their three children.

In Tobruk, Libya, I do not recall how I met the head of police, who acted somewhat like the mayor. He spoke limited English but enough for some conversation. Hearing of my professed interest in learning more about countries and cultures from their personal point of view, he rather challenged me to see such life from inside a harem—his.

Might not any woman reasonably suspect that such an invitation was only a thinly disguised ruse to achieve some sexual conquest? I half wondered as much but stated explicitly that such ideas were out of the question. He assured me that I would be safe, just some anthropological study—he actually used that wording. I wonder how many women would have believed him? I did, and he was a man of his word.

So how did I find life in a harem, in *purdah*? I suppose I expected signs of jealousy or hostility between the two wives. On the contrary, as far as I could tell, they were very friendly with each other.

I felt narrowed—confined or imprisoned—by the gate that the man locked behind him upon going out to work. As far as I could tell the wives did not share my sentiment. If they had any feeling at all about that high wall, I thought it might be relief at feeling protected from whatever might lie beyond the gate. No would-be violators could break in on them.

We had not a word of verbal communication among us. So I was left to surmise their feelings. My suppositions would, of course, be somewhat influenced by the inescapable tendency to project our own feelings onto others around us. Even if we had been able to converse, hearing their feelings would have required the assumption that they could communicate them and that they would be honest about them if they recognized them.

So were these two wives "happy"? That might not be the relevant question. Happiness, according to Aristotle, is not a light, emotional state, transitory and vulnerable to external circumstances, but the development of a deeper sense of "goodness" within the soul or psyche. Happiness is considered an end in itself, as the final achievement of right and true acts. As far as I can discern from my very limited acquaintance with human history, happiness was not a concept connected with acquisition of things until Thomas Jefferson changed John Locke's thoughts about property and reworded them to be "the pursuit of happiness." Before that people lived aware of evil in the world, trying their best to do right acts to appease the divine controller of human affairs in order to avoid calamities that might be sent as divine retribution for wrong action. They interpreted the absence of disasters or the presence of favorable cropping conditions and such as signs of the favor of the controller of human destiny.

"Happiness," as we generally consider the term since Jefferson has become very much in vogue in the so-called advanced nations and as such, might motivate the question whether the two wives were happy. We must ask whether the idea of happiness in this sense has not given rise to unrealistic

expectations that cannot be met, the failure to attain those expectations resulting in considerable human unhappiness that is avoided if we never think in
terms of happiness or the pursuit of happiness in the first place.

Is my thinking along this line influenced or even determined by some little acquaintance from the Buddhist belief that desire is the cause of misery?
Maybe. I had read about some such Buddhist concepts decades before I just
had to go see for myself how such concepts came out in practice.

So as far as I could see (which admittedly was hardly at all), these plural
wives were content enough that it never occurred to them to rebel against their
situation, just as people seemed content in the system of Communism as I saw
it in operation in the Soviet Union. Yet that system was gone just three decades
after I was there, though not so much from rebellion by those whom the system
was victimizing as much as the weight of their failed economic system.

It has been four decades since my glimpse of *purdah* life in the Muslim world.
For all I know, *purdah* may be disappearing or on the decline in most parts of
the world, but we all know that it was rampant in a most virulent form in
Afghanistan until recently. The strictest ideal of *purdah* holds that the female
leaves her home only twice in her life: the first time to go from father or male
protector to husband and the second time carried feet first in a shroud to either
burial or to a burning ghat.

We tend to see the wearing of *burqa*s whether by custom or law as repressive, but I have not read about the even greater repression of *purdah*. By
comparison *burqa* wearing seems to me to be like a partial *purdah*, a step up
toward "modernity" and less restriction from strict *purdah* in which the women
were confined within their own—that is their male quasi-owner's—home.

We hear a lot about "informed consent" in this country and I recently
had to sign some documents about that. I wondered how "informed" I could
possibly be as I signed in what I knew was at deep level real ignorance. I am
supposed to be reasonably intelligent and well educated. I suspected that most
who supposed themselves "informed" were even more ignorant than I am
without even realizing their ignorance.

Qui tacet consentiret: "Silence implies consent," so says Sir Thomas
Moore. But can we view the silence of Muslim women as a sign of their consent to this way of life when they know no other way? How could anyone
who from birth had been sheltered away from knowledge of the outside
world, living inside a rather pleasant home and courtyard surrounded by *much*
loving attention from mother and friendly attention from other women until
puberty, *possibly* be "informed"

I thought I saw very healthy infant and early childhood interactions with adults in the household where *purdah* was practiced. The man also had a daughter who was about fourteen years old. Her mother was dead. The two wives each had one child, one a toddling girl and one infant boy. True, I was never in a like situation with a Western woman and her child for two days with no means of communication, but I cannot think they could lavish as much attention on their infants as these mothers did.

Why not? They had no interruptions: no phone calls, no need to shop for groceries, no soap operas. Their only responsibility was to keep the place neat—and it was neat as a pin—and do minimal cooking on two small camp-like stoves. With two grown women and one girl nearly grown, what else was there to do day after day but play with the infants and children?

Besides playing with the infants and children, how else did these women occupy their time? After all, not much time is needed for three (the daughter worked alongside the wives) vigorous young women to keep a small house neat. All three did elaborate embroidery.

The husband alternated nights with his wives. The wife whose night it was prepared a more elaborate meal on her stove between cuddling her child, while the other wife prepared a simpler meal for herself and the stepdaughter. When the husband came in, a small table was pulled to center of his bedroom, and he indicated for me to eat with him as that wife served. The toddler was in the room or running in and out on nights his mother spent with the husband. When the infant's mother took her turn, the infant was in an elaborate cradle at the foot of the bed when not being cuddled by his father.

I learned that the chief concern of the husband at that time was finding a suitable husband for his daughter now that she was of marriageable age. I am sure he was like the majority of parents or fathers in such arranged marriages, though some fathers would have entirely different criteria of "suitable," such as those who were eager to engage the man offering the highest bride price. Thankfully, to prevent that type of abuse of the system, I had the impression the bride price was fairly well set.

The husband related to me that he did take satisfaction in his having paid more for his younger wife than for the slightly older one because she had attended school. That indicated to me that he valued some education for a woman, yet he had kept his daughter in *purdah* rather than sending her to school. By "suitable" he did consider financial stability and the likelihood that the potential husband be a "good provider" and from a good family. In general this father, like fathers everywhere, wanted to find someone likely to be a good, stable, solid husband likely to please his daughter and provide for her.

Love? Whatever love is, this man viewed it as the result, not cause, of a good marriage. I found the same attitude prevalent in the Hindu world of India, too, where arranged marriage was still common when I was there.

By a "good marriage," I understood them to mean a generally satisfactory life for both partners marked by realistic contentment, though not necessarily by some unrealistic fairytale about "happily ever after."

Such had been the character of this man's marriage to his first wife of some years. When she died, left with a still-small daughter, he needed another wife to care for the child. He took two. He did not say so, but I gathered the first marriage had been arranged for him and that while it was satisfactory, he also could not afford more than one wife at that time.

By the time of his second and third marriages, he was financially established and did his own arranging, although neither wife did her own negotiating. He did not say so, but I got the impression that taking even more wives would be permissible if he desired to do so, but he had not.

This situation that I witnessed seemed surely to have been a case of voluntary *purdah* for the young second wife, as she had been out of *purdah* enough for some school, surely at the time becoming literate in Arabic. The power of expectation and other psychological forms of coercion, however, were impossible for me to measure.

Now that this young woman was relegated to *purdah*, in the absence of any reading, I wondered how much time would pass before she lapsed into illiteracy. Would she never again read for the rest of her life? Perhaps. But I think maybe change might come to the culture, allowing her more exposure to the written word. Unfortunately though, with modernism has also come a sharp rise in reactionary fundamentalism in both Western and Muslim countries, perhaps Hindu and Buddhist societies also. With the unrest and "freeing" by force happening in those parts of the world now, how the future will play out for these women is uncertain.

In that Libyan home, I saw nothing at all symbolic of religion. I knew that Islam forbids making or displaying pictures of animate beings or representation of the Prophet, as they believe angels will not enter a home with pictures (or dogs) and the picture maker will burn in hell. Neither did I expect a copy of the Qu'ran in every home, as our image of even the most backward log cabin home on the United States' frontier had a Bible. But in a home where life was so ruled by religious custom, not seeing any visual symbolism of the religion was notable.

In *purdah* some might find such nothing-to-do boredom to bring its own stress and discontent instead of peace. As far as I could tell, the wives did not. Nor did I, although the situation was somewhat artificial because I knew I could leave any time the man came home.

I do not know anything else to remark about what I considered a remarkable short stay in a harem. I think I had expected some startling insight or tedious boredom. I found neither. Instead, I found, with the help of a typically hospitable Arabic man, an opportunity to understand a bit more about the practice of Islam. In the face of the wives being unable to communicate a single word, I hope that I am not now more first-handedly misunderstanding or misconstruing than before.

☙❧

At one point I sailed from Calcutta to Rangoon across the Bay of Bengal on a Pacific and Orient liner. At one stop in Chittagong, the women stayed aboard ship, but many men disembarked, and all seemed to be smokers but not puffing. Then I heard the *muezzin* and a strange, even astounding, phenomenon before my eyes—every man put his cigarette in his mouth and started puffing. At the same time, I saw the red ball of the sun just sinking below the horizon and it hit me—Ramadan! And with sunset it was now permissible, the fast being over, to smoke. Thus a very visible practice of Islam, the Ramadan, a month-long fast prohibiting food, water, cigarettes, or sex between sunrise and sunset, was being strictly observed.

I wonder how much peer pressure played a role in observance of Ramadan. Among all those men, one who smoked during the day would be very noticeable. In the Muslim world, more Westernized Muslims may center on a nuclear family, leaving a single adult home alone for part of the day, as the couple whose apartment in Turkey I visited. Among such women alone at their homes such peer pressure might be not so strong. To drink water, tea, or juice—Islam strictly prohibits alcohol and port at all times—during the day during Ramadan might pass unnoticed. In most places though, I think a more extended family constellation or polygamy is still common, if not prevalent. In households with several adults present most of the time, peer pressure not to break the fast might be stronger.

For me, to fast from food from sunrise to sunset would not be onerous, as I should think I could eat a hearty predawn meal (and go back to bed?) and eat again after sunset. But fasting from drinking water would be very hard for me; I should think even Muslim medical personnel would admit refraining from water is not healthy.

So why did Allah command such a prolonged fast? "On no soul doth Allah place a burden greater than it can bear," says the Qu'ran. Allah wants us to be happy. If some burden is just too much, the believers do not have to bear, if I read the Qu'ran rightly (which I make no claim to do). How does the requirement for such extreme fasting reconcile with the more compassionate image of Allah gleaned from the Qu'ran passage?

For that matter, some Christians fast as a part of their religious devotion, citing Christ's fast as their example. But Christian Testament has Jesus saying that he came to give more abundant life to the world. Is it more abundant to *fast*? If not done to the point of malnourishment, fasting might make the breakfast more enjoyable, I suppose.

I do not know about Buddhist monks who eschew afternoon rice (not morning rice though) in religious devotion or any Hindu fast practices, though there is quite a bit of that; Mahatma Gandhi's fasts are famous. But his were not to please any deity, as I understand it, but intended to be a consciousness-raising technique for the British to bring about change in the political system.

Does Ramadan also have that aspect? I do not know that it does. But it appears that Ramadan is an act of restraint to show devotion to Allah or his desires coupled with the apparently contradictory value that it is good for human beings be happy.

That may not be as contradictory as it seems. Can human beings achieve happiness without exercising some restraint? The difference seems to hinge on the voluntariness of the action, whether coerced deprivation or self-sacrifice, whether imposed from without or personally chosen from within, is the crucial factor. Unless *too* extreme, fasting or other restraints may indeed bring us joy, not from masochism, but from healthy self-congratulation at doing a hard thing and from our belief that we have pleased the believed-in Power.

༺༻

My second "experiencing" of Ramadan was very different from seeing a street full of men whip out cigarettes at sunset.

When our ship landed at Yongon, the first thing I had to do was find shelter. I hoped to find suitable accommodations for a stay of a few days. I found a hotel that appeared to meet my needs and secured a room there.

A sizable number of East and West Pakistani immigrants resided in Yongon. It turned out the proprietor of the hotel was Muslim. A common area was set up to provide multiple meals. I thought that it must be a gathering place for several Muslims—men, women, and children—to gather after sunset to feast and party all night long until the last food, water, tea, and juice was gone just before sunrise, when they would stagger off to bed. After all my contemplation about the nature of the fasting, it was a startling sight for me to see Ramadan not as fast but as *feast*.

Were these Yongon Muslim Ramadan feasters making a travesty of what I supposed was the purpose of Ramadan? Did their feasting somehow interfere with their meditation on how to become a better or more holy Muslim or their intent to lead a more holy life?

At first, I thought so. But Allah the Compassionate would surely want his believers to be happy, despite their having to fast during the day for a month. I thought consciously or not they were observing the other strand of Islam, and I suppose one found in most religions: Besides fasting on occasion, the Deity desires overall that human beings be happy. Practicing restraint is for the purpose of increasing happiness, blessedness in the long run, whether in this world or the next life.

I concluded that the Yongon daytime Ramadan fasters were hoping to achieve happiness and avoid hellfire in the next life, while the nighttime feasters were hoping to achieve joy in this life. Both intents followed Allah as revealed to the prophet Mohammed.

&

In Pakistan I asked a young woman her notion of the best thing about Islam. She had a ready answer: "Freedom—it leaves us to be free." I have pondered these nearly forty years since what she meant by that.

I could dimly recognize some aspects of freedom behind the *burqa* veil, such as automatic modesty no matter how feet and legs are arranged. But today's Western women's ordinary wearing of slacks have at last made us free in that respect without the restraints of Islam.

Then, in that brief harem stay, I thought of my time there hazily as "free" in the same sense that an ocean voyage temporarily frees us from the stress, strain, and hassle of our ordinary daily rat race so that we can focus on the joy of just being alive. While I was there for those few days, I had not a care in the world and no responsibility whatsoever for that brief time.

Mind you, I was a trifle concerned over some things. Suppose a fire broke out with us locked in? Or suppose the man dropped dead and never came home? Suppose he were a vicious type who just tired of his life and left someday? Apparently, these doubts did not occur to his wives, though I had no way of finding out their fears if they had any.

Free? I thought of one of Franklin Roosevelt's four essential human freedoms—freedom from fear: for example, from fear that your work for wages might be judged lacking, or if so, and you lost your job, that you might never again find another. If these wives had had any notion the husband might lose his job, causing them to become destitute, I could not tell. They simply seemed to depend on him, utterly *trusting* in him, for all matters.

In the Muslim world, men appeared to enjoy sexual freedom because even where monogamy is law, there appears to be more availability of additional partners for men. In the polygamous situation, wives appeared to me to have a certain sort of sexual freedom, too, in not having to provide such intense sexual pleasure—just having to provide release and children, preferably sons.

In those senses I thought that I could understand the woman's finding that for her the best thing of Islam is the freedom it gives. But is that what she meant? I just do not know.

Why did I not pursue what she did mean? I do not know that either, but I think because sometimes when I am trying to find out more about an opinion, the person whom I am questioning adopts a sort of frustrated defensive posture and begins arguing as though he or she perceives me to be criticizing instead of only inquiring, which is the last thing I want to do.

Abroad I was even more careful to try to avoid that than I am in the United States, supposing that since we share a common language here, the person questioned would better understand my intention.

Of all my learning about the Muslim world, to me this one statement from a *burqa*-wearing Muslim woman that a good thing about Islam is that it frees, holds the most significance to me, causing me to think about her meaning ever since.

STUDY QUESTIONS

1. The author traveled to the Muslim world between 1956 and 1960. She appears to have had quite positive perceptions of the people then.
- Do you think the author's perception of the Muslim world might be different today after the attacks on the United States in 2001?

2. While wearing a *burqa*, the author heard American military personnel making crude sexual comments about her. She says, "I was quite amused."
- Had these soldiers made the same comments while she was wearing Western style dress, would the author have been so amused?
- How does this attitude compare with the "proper lady" self-image described by the author elsewhere in the book?

4. The author says "In the polygamous situation, wives appeared to me to have a certain sort of sexual freedom, too, in not having to provide such intense sexual pleasure—just being required to provide release and children."
- Does this assessment sound like a reasonable understanding of the positions of women in polygamous situations?
- How does this attitude compare with the author's self-report of being opposed to subjugation of women?

5. A Muslim women who wore the *burqa* said that for her the best thing about Islam was freedom. The author described her time in *purdah* as free of stress and the wives as content. Then she wondered what would happen to them if fire broke out or if the husband never returned while they were locked in.
- How do you account for this apparent concurrent contradiction?
- What evidence did the author have upon which to base her conclusion that the harem wives appeared content?
- What do you think the Pakistani woman meant by saying Islam left her to be free?

Six

NATURAL WONDERS

Though "natural wonders" sounds more like a conventional travelogue than a personal memoir, many of my recollections focus on the amazing natural geography that I had the privilege to see in the course of my travels. In deciding which sites to tour, the list of UNESCO World Heritage Sites was very helpful. In public libraries have descriptions of these sites in vivid color.

On the other hand, I never tried to preview sites by researching books before my travels. I regret that in a way, but in many cases the opportunities arose after I arrived. Had I waited to pre-study, the opportunities may have passed by without my ever getting another. Life is too short to pass up opportunity as we find them.

Beyond joy at the unexpected, at a deeper level I attribute my failure to study extensively before travel to the fear of death, unique to human beings among animals. For me, less than the fear of dying is my acute sense of the brevity of time we have for living. If I took too long to study beforehand, my precious opportunity to "see for myself" might be lost. I infinitely prefer direct experience to a pale imitation in any representational medium.

That being said, I am haunted by wondering if I have exploited this lofty need to "see for myself" as a stalling device for any duty to "achieve" myself, to repay the human lives that made my life possible. Possibly this memoir is a fumbling attempt to do that.

Since the convention in compiling lists of wonders has used the Pythagoras' "perfect" number seven so often, I have compiled a list of the "Seven Greatest Natural Wonders of the World" that I have personally seen.

ॐॐ

Iguaçu Falls of the Iguaçu River is located where Paraguay, Argentina, and Brazil meet. Before traveling to Paraguay, I was not aware of ever hearing of the falls. Perhaps it was not on the UNESCO list then as it was later. People I met there told me that I must not leave without seeing this great wonder. Luckily, I was on my way to Brazil, and the falls was on the way.

What a *stupendous* sight!—far beyond any words of anybody: more than merely beautiful, more than merely powerful and awesome, more than breathtaking, a sort of mind-taking. I just could not get my mind around Iguaçu or find words to match the magnificence. I think that being entirely unexpected, serendipitous experience intensified its impact on me.

The day I arrived was rainy and dark. I was so amazed that I could not even imagine the greatness in sparkling sunlight or full moonlight.

I vacillated between staying over another day, hoping to view the falls again in sunshine, and reluctantly continuing on my way on business. The urge to see it again won out and I returned to the falls on the afternoon and night of the full moon. The experience in sunshine was even more stupendous than in the rain, making me glad for my decision to cut what now seemed like paltry business by comparison.

Looking forward to moonlit viewing later, I prepared myself to drink it in all night on a comfortable bench with a good view.

Oh, the inexpressible joy of my full moon viewing. For a while.

My joy was shattered by three bellhops from the hotel there who planted themselves between the bench and edge, totally blocking my view. They tried to carry on inane talk with me in very limited English, Spanish, or what I guessed was their native Portuguese, all the while blocking my view.

Grrrr!

Sure, I knew they were simply trying to be "kind" not only to spare me from what they thought was my state of being lonesome, but also to offer me a place in one of their rooms. They offered to double up if I could not afford the hotel, which they concluded was the only reason anyone would spend the night on a bench when nights are for sleeping, never dreaming.

Hoping they would go away, I tried to be as minimally communicative as possible. I wanted to enjoy the view all night long, especially because it was a once-in-a-lifetime opportunity, whereas I could spend practically the whole rest of my life sleeping.

Would it have been justifiable homicide to push them over the cliff?

Eventually they left me in peace to relish that glorious view.

I pondered how this marvel is so remote from the world that we usually think of as "world." So very few people of the world could ever see it, only those of affluence, or as I was then, not affluent, but having business nearby. I felt so fortunate and blessed to have been given this experience.

I must have caught the great Iguaçu Falls just after a very rainy year or more that made for an almighty rush of water because I read long after that after a long drought there might be only a trickle—not any natural wonder at all—this mighty wonder that was the unrivaled top of my listing of natural wonders! I smile to think that like Fujiyama, Iguaçu put on a show just for me.

Next thing I knew, the bright sun was shining on Iguaçu and on me. To my chagrin, I realized that I had fallen asleep. I could not blame the bellhops for that!

I longed to remain, but the exigencies of ordinary life compelled me to leave the grand falls of Iguaçu—but with such a *great* memory!

Later I recalled I *had* heard about this marvel through the eyes, mind, and pen of Richard Halliburton, favorite author of my childhood. His adventures might have been a, if not *the*, major impetus that made me years later experience many such marvels for myself, even to the idea of sleeping at the wonder for whatever deeper experiencing, for Halliburton frequently did that. I made a mental note to reread Halliburton after returning home, but as usual with such resolves to study more about it later, later has not come yet but maybe still will.

࠾ᦇ

As the second of my greatest wonders I list Pamulkale in central Turkey. On a Christian religious pilgrimage in the mid-1990s, although Pamulkale was not on the pre-set itinerary because it was not known to be of biblical significance, after arriving, we found that for some reason Miletus, where Paul said farewell to the elders according to Acts, was impractical to visit, so we went to Pamulkale as an alternative.

Again delightful serendipity intervened to bring me great joy!

A great, smooth, glacial-like expanse of limestone, white yet sparkling with color, glints in the sun. The name Pamulkale means "white castle" or "white palace." Hot springs bubble out of the ground with a load of salts, which upon contact with cooler air congeal to this white stone, travertine. Centuries of build-up have created the splendor there today. I understand that for many centuries some kind of balance of the springs' outpouring of salts and evaporation has resulted in the area remaining much as it looked two millennia ago.

We are fortunate that today wonderful photographs are readily available to illustrate the wondrousness that I find impossible to describe with words.

I think that Pamulkale ranks high on my list because of my bias toward locations of biblical interest. As I gazed I thought, *"This* is John of Patmos' 'great white throne' of God and the Lamb!" for the place is fairly near the semicircle of those seven congregations in Asia Minor to whom John wrote the seven letters documented in the first chapters of Revelations.

How much I would have missed without ever knowing I had missed anything at all had our intended itinerary not been diverted!

࠾ᦇ

The Andes Mountains nearly ranked at the head of my list instead of third, and if Igauçu has no rivals for first place, the Andes tied with Pamulkale for next. I think one reason Pamulkale edged over it was how I could "see" the white castle throne in the travertine, but no one can "see" the Andes, for the range stretches over the entire continent of South America from north to south—far beyond the scope of human vision in one glance. So I could marvel at only a small part of the range and then another and another, yet other parts seemed to go on forever.

I traveled down the Andes range from northern Columbia through the Cordilleras, Oriental to the east and Occidental to the west, with the Altiplano in between—I was on both—as far south as Arica, Chile, for some fifteen months (not continuously). Still, I never saw the wonder in all. I think no one ever could. That is along its length. But crossing the Andes from east to west takes only two or three days by bus and that is how I more nearly "saw" the Andes.

From the Pacific coast the Andes rise sharply in elevation. Each of the times that I made partial crossings, such as through Canon del Pato, Paso del condor, or on the train from Bolivia to Chile, I started inland, already quite high up among them, through passes among the highest peaks.

As with all of the great mountain ranges, the passes are used for transportation or other uses practical for human beings, whereas the peaks seem to satisfy some sort of yearning to experience their indescribable awesome grandeur, to acknowledge the aesthetics, sometimes to satisfy religious instincts, and sometimes to satisfy the human need to conquer a challenge.

I never heard whether the ancient Andeans ever considered any peaks of the Andes sacred, but then there is so much more of what I have never heard than that of which I have. But the Lake of the Andes, Lake Titicaca, was sacred to ancient Andeans.

Unlike Iguaçu Falls or Pamulkale, of course I had "known of" the Andes long before I experienced them. But "know" them? Not at all. Not even after being there. Not having traveled among them. Too much to know!

Every encyclopedia has several pages about the Andes. Anyone can look up such articles. But ordinary words cannot scratch the surface. Even poetic words fall short. Come to think of it, I do not recall any whole mountain range as the subject of a poem, or any peaks the subject of poetry. But peaks inspire religious imagining as thrusting toward the sky or "heaven" to meet Divinity.

American landscape painter Frederic Edwin Church put his brush on them. After I had experienced the Andes, I was amazed to view his great rendering of parts of them, especially in "Heart of the Andes" and "Cotopaxi." I was lucky enough to see both the Andes and the original Church paintings.

These works are so great, for me to even think to write my own memoir of the Andes—or any other wonder—is presumptuous, but here I am doing it anyhow. I wondered whether Church felt presumptuous as he painted the Andes' "heart." If he did, I am glad that he persevered nonetheless.

My two favorite peaks of the Andes are Illiami and Illampu, not far from La Paz. They formed the magnificent view out the window of the small hotel at which I stayed several times in La Paz. After the first time, I always asked for the same room.

Truly, no words, photographs, or even Churchian paintings can get the heart of the whole Andes range, only some part of it.

❧

Mount Fujiyama ranks high in my priority because of a bias from my childhood. My favorite picture in my favorite book, my blue third-grade geography
book, was of snowcapped Fujiyama, like a sweet, smooth, vanilla ice cream
cone—upside down. As a child I never had any thought of actually seeing for
myself some day the marvels depicted in that cherished old book.

Ironically, my actual viewing lasted only a very few minutes. But the
events that led up to my seeing it, climaxed by those brief minutes, account
for how wonderful my experience there was.

I had been abroad nearly the whole year of 1960–1961. Now I was on
my way home again by necessity because, unlike Richard Halliburton, for me
travel was not a money-making career. On my way from Hong Kong to San
Francisco, I took a seventy-two-hour transit visa to stopover in Japan with the
specific objective of seeing Fujiyama and then whatever else of Japan I could
crowd into seventy-two hours.

What a very great bargain that stopover was! I had never before or since
experienced such a great deal in so short a time.

When the plane landed in Tokyo, the clock started ticking for me. Since
Fuji was my main priority, I got the information about it at the YWCA hotel
and planned to take early train scheduled for the next morning. I knew that
many Japanese and others climb Fuji, as they consider it one of the sacred
mounts on the globe. That aspect did not apply to me, as I am enthralled by
mountains as mountains, not for sacredness. I would have dearly loved to
climb also, but I knew time would not permit and I was in Japan in spring,
when the weather can make for treacherous climbing conditions.

For some reason I do not recall, my trip to Fuji was postponed until the
following day. So I toured Tokyo on the first day. I took a commercial general
city tour and the operator or guide said that since I was American, the language would be English. Feeling guilty that this bus full of Japanese people
would have to forego their language for mine, I apologized to them. One
spoke up, "That's all right, lady, we do not speak Japanese either. We are
from California!" A distinctly American-sounding chuckle followed. The way
the guide had directed her statement to me, she seemed to have taken the other
passengers for Japanese instead of Americans also.

The highlight of Tokyo for me was finding a miniature Japanese garden.
I knew the Japanese are famous for their love of natural beauty and the art of
the miniature, such as bonsai trees.

I had been walking along the Ginza when I noticed a wooden door in a
wall with people passing in and out. After observing to make sure that some of
the people were women, to avoid stumbling into a men's rest room, I followed
a woman in. I found myself in a garden no bigger than a large room. Five conifers formed the forest. A tiny brook, evidently supplied by a hidden hose from

a faucet, gurgled happily—or should I say that the gurgling brook made the people in the garden happier—calmer and more serene. A tiny bridge arched the tiny stream, reminding me of blue willow-ware china. A path of stepping stones in the grass led to two benches in the center of this garden gem.

That night I had another thrill at a Japanese country inn. I was looking forward, albeit with some trepidation, to mixed-gender bathing, Japanese style. I think the managers thought that would be too great a culture shock for me. I think that they closed off the bath to others while I bathed, for I was the only one there. Having learned in India that the procedure for the bath is not to sit in the water and wash, but to sit on the edge and dip water to wet oneself, soap up, and then dip to splash over oneself to rinse, the smiling young woman guide expressed admiration that I already knew the correct way.

It was the bedding mound for sleeping that I loved—much more comfortable sleeping on the floor than when I flung a sleeping bag on the ground or a bare floor when no alternative was available. Then the hosts brought in the foot-high (or less?) dining table. In Japanese tradition, I sat on floor to eat the several small bowls of food. I was getting to experience "the real Japan" and the big Fujiyama view I had come for was still to come!

Up early the next morning to an unfortunately gray, foggy day with practically no visibility, I found that even such dismal weather could not hide the glory of cherry blossom time as I walked along the road out to where I was told would be the best viewing spot for Fujiyama—if the clouds would lift and sun come out. All I could do was hope for the weather to clear.

In a little while I found the spot and made myself comfortable. From that vantage point I could not see a thing but the beauty of cherry blossoms practically in my face because fog obliterated the mountain entirely. I was near tears!

I tried to console myself with the beauty of the blossoms and the good walk along the road, all the while forming a desperate plan: I would wait there all day if necessary and if the weather never did clear enough to reveal the mountain view, I would return to that country inn and try again on the third day, since I calculated that I would still have time by dark to take the train back to Tokyo and catch the midnight plane—when my visa would expire—for San Francisco.

So I waited—and waited. Then, quite suddenly, the cloud veil lifted to reveal a marvelous view of this perfect cone-capped volcanic mountain—no wonder so revered by Japanese! I shared their reverence at that moment.

Then the most astounding thing happened. As suddenly as the cloud veil had lifted, it lowered, again blotting the view entirely. As I said, the entire experience lasted but a few short minutes, but those perfect few minutes rank among the greatest, if not even being *the* greatest, highlights of my life.

I felt as though I had experienced some semi-mystic ecstasy, as if the entire universe had staged a show for me alone. Indescribable!

Although pleasurable, after that spectacular view of Fujiyama, the rest of my time in Tokyo was a bit anticlimactic. I made the flight with fifteen minutes to spare to get the transit visa stamped and board the plane. All the passengers seemed to be Americans and sort of burst into a glad rendition of "California Here We Come!" Like me, they all seemed—happy to travel to see the wonders of the world, yes, but—oh, so glad to be going home again!

෨৵৶

Listed after, but almost in a dead heat with, Fujiyama, I put the Big Trees of California, the giant sequoias. One reason the trees so impressed me is that they are *alive*, even still growing, instead of geologic wonders of nature.

I slept in a grove of the Big Trees. Unlike my night at Iguaçu, if anyone even noticed me, they must have thought that my action was just a natural way to better appreciate these awesome giants. They were so huge that even craning my neck I could not take in a whole tree at once but had to walk around to try to see one more fully.

The bed of redwood needles under my sleeping bag was soft and delightful. The scent was subtle and pleasing. For such giant pines to grow from thumb-sized cones is awesome. Of course, they do not grow from cones but from seeds in the cone. I have never been able to pick out seeds from a cone and could not from these. Still, seeing the cones was such a marvel. I have some sugar pine cones some ten inches long that produce only average-size trees by comparison.

More than the giant size and beauty of these trees, I am enchanted by their age. Some of these specimens were the oldest living things on the entire planet—awe-inspiring beyond words.

To think that these would be seedlings when people were building Stonehenge or the Nubian pyramids, big trees, but not yet "the Big Trees" during the Crusades! Had they reached full growth when Christopher Columbus sailed? I think they had by the time Thomas Jefferson penned previously unvoiced human yearnings for self-government.

Later I learned that bristlecone pines atop the arid mountains of the Great Basin from Colorado to California are the oldest living things on Earth, the Big Trees being second oldest. I have seen bristlecone pines. Much older, perhaps, but the way they grow spread out but quite short to me did not hold a candle to the so tall, *tall*, big-around, perfect, majestic proportion and grandeur of the Big Trees of California.

෨৵৶

When I went into my memory bank for the seven *greatest* of all the great natural wonders I have seen on our great planet Earth, Lake Titicaca naturally fell in sixth place. It was not until thinking to write about it that I realized it was already there, so to speak, mentioned as the Lake of the Andes. No matter, here it is even if that makes the Andes make the list implicitly again.

Beautiful, yes, both in afternoon daylight and later in glittering starlight. But I think Titicaca is memorable to me for another of our senses. The bitter cold there drove me into the warmth of sleeping bag and covers until daylight again. So this was awesome to the tactile sense, not touch with the fingers as such, but over my whole self: a bitter, shivery, invigorating *cold*. I have tried to recall other experiences of coldness that might qualify to me as invigorating, but this ranked beyond all others.

Could I not have felt the same wondrous iciness other places?

I tried to re-feel Titicaca's cold splendor in other situations out of the Andes and among them, such as at the top of Paso del condor. Even compared to places that were colder in measurable terms, the sense of being amid that vast expanse of water was unique. I never felt that type of coldness in any other place or at any other time.

A look-up in my beloved book of color photographs and brief, factual descriptions of "Wonders of the World" said that Lake Titicaca is only the second-largest lake in South America, Lake Maracaibo in Venezuela, if considered a lake, being larger. (Since Maracaibo is connected by a strait to the Gulf of Venezuela, and by that to the Caribbean Ocean, some definitions would consider it a sea.)

I saw Maracaibo but was so unimpressed that I had to think about it in order to even recall the experience. I have no need to spend effort to recall any of the natural wonders on my list, though, because I can never forget them. More than just a part of my mind—my memory—my experiences at those wonders have become a part of my life, my self.

Maracaibo having been so insignificant to me despite being the largest lake in South America and having the book already open, my insatiable curiosity compelled me to read more. No one else listing wonders considered this body of water much of a natural wonder either. That made me realize that size alone was not what made the Andes or the Big Trees great wonders.

Then what does qualify a natural formation as a wonder?

For me, the most significant factor is subjectivity. In many cases, a great number of people share the same sense of greatness about the same places or things, if not to the identical degree or with regard to minor details. While subjective, the phenomenon cannot be merely an idiosyncratic judgment.

Mere hype—marketing by the tourist industry—cannot account for the attraction either. Some people will spend considerable resources to travel to see wonders rarely mentioned by advertisements and in places quite off the beaten path of the typical tourist.

Perhaps it is in our nature to think if these places are pleasing to the Divinity, then by visiting these places we share a spiritual experience and somehow even merge with the Divinity, becoming sacred ourselves. Some might believe that these features of nature are evidence of a Creator. No wonder the ancients considered Titicaca sacred; I do, too, whatever "sacred" means.

అంఴ

What did I choose as the seventh of the seven? I had a very difficult choice between Crater Lake in Oregon and Khyber Pass in the Hindu Kush Mountains connecting the northern frontier of Pakistan with Afghanistan.

Crater Lake edged out by a hair.

What is so wonderful about Crater Lake? Beauty, of course. But its beauty lies beyond just beauty as with every natural wonder on my list. Power, majesty, words beyond wonder? Yes. For me and for any of my acquaintances who have also experienced it.

Nearly 7,000 years ago, the cone of a great volcano, Mount Mazama, collapsed creating the lake, one of the world's best-known calderas. Another smaller volcanic cone rising from within the lake has formed a small island with its own perfect little cone, though not snowcapped when I was there. Thus, Crater Lake is like Mount Fujiama with its cap inverted.

The water in the lake is indescribable. Anyone can read a technical description in any library, but verbal descriptions are inadequate to the task. I must be content to record my appreciation of the wonder for which I have no words to convey. I so *appreciated* these natural wonders that this memoir may be taken as a "token of my appreciation."

అంఴ

In addition to my personal seven great wonders of the world, many other natural wonders stand out in my mind. Some readers might wonder why Victoria Falls situated between Zimbabwe (formerly Rhodesia) and Zambia, Africa, did not rank "top seven" listing. Had it been "top ten," the falls would have been on it, I think.

Victoria's famous rainbow effect has more *color* than others I have ever seen. To me it appeared almost a pastel pink. Victoria also seemed to me to be higher and wider than Niagara Falls. I was awed that its might and power went on and on and *on* for so many millions of years and was likely to continue far into the future.

Near all of the great great waterfalls I heard a grand roar beyond a roar that overwhelmed the senses but was not assaultive or frightening. I thought that even a blind person might experience a thrill from waterfalls, for their roar, loud or soft, is never noise, but music to my ears. The same holds true for the sound of pounding surf against a shore.

Amazing how a small, spherical brain can hold such a huge cargo of containers full of such memoirs!

STUDY QUESTIONS

1. In the introduction to this chapter, the author says, "Life is too short to pass up opportunities as we find them."
- Discuss the author's balance between taking charge of her travels with a plan and seizing serendipitous opportunities as she found them. Do you think that her planning influenced what unexpected opportunities she found?
- Discuss how life planning in general can influence serendipity.
- "Some guys have all the luck." Do you think that there is a way to favorably influence the "luck" you have?

2. In this chapter the author uses the words sacred, biblical significance, Divinity, spiritual, and sacred, "whatever 'sacred' means."
- Using this chapter as a starting point, what do you think that the author means by sacred?
- Do you think that this author believes in a supreme deity that is behind all creation?

3. The author states, "I so appreciated these natural wonders that this memoir may be taken as a 'token of my appreciation.'"
- Does the word "appreciation" imply a person to whom the appreciation is felt?
- Discuss what you think that the author meant by "appreciation."

Seven

BUILT WONDERS

As I did with the natural wonders, I have selected list of seven built wonders that had the greatest impact on me. Why seven? Perhaps to show solidarity with the human race that long before me seemed to evince a strong affinity with the number seven—seeking communion with Divinity perhaps? Many of these built wonders represent just that, a collective seeking of human communion with Divinity.

Great as all the natural wonders of our planet are, I find even greater the built wonders engineered by human beings throughout history. No human genius, will, blood, sweat, and tears were necessary to achieve the natural wonders that so thrill the heart. Because I share in their humanity, in a way I feel that I share in those built wonders. My heart swells with pride to know that my fellow human beings built them.

Still, thoughts of the great cost in human effort that the massive projects required to complete them make me sad. Such great expenditure of effort: given voluntarily? Against their will? For what? Is it true that some very powerful rulers compelled necessary labor to build funerary structures because of their fear of what they believed about life after death? If what they believed about life after death is true, does that mean that those laborers too poor or powerless to acquire their own pyramids will be doomed for eternity after death?

So while I appreciate the wonders, I keep in mind the human costs. I appreciate the collective social or political will that was necessary to build them. These great marvels may be the lasting human heritage of individual genius in conception, but realizing the individual dream required many, sometimes thousands, of individual workers' collective effort.

I wonder if the crews worked voluntarily, or if they were at the mercy of controlling forces. Even if they worked voluntarily, I am convinced that there was no "free choice," only the option to choose the lesser of what seems to me to be evils. They seemed to have a fierce desire to please the gods and they believed their rulers were the representatives of the gods on Earth. Thus, they could choose a life of hard labor or risk loss of love of the gods. In turn, pleasing the gods meant pleasing their rulers.

"Love" here may not be the word for what I feel or felt on seeing these great built wonders, but love is the nearest I can come to describe some inner emotion that humans have, inspiring them to do some work, great or small, beyond fear of physical punishment as consequence for avoiding the work.

Yet even as I thought of the cost in human effort, even at the cost of loss of life in some cases, I could not resist the thought, "Oh, it was *worth* the cost to create this marvel, this great built wonder!"

৯৽৽৾৾

By my way of thinking, the Taj Mahal has no rival whatever for first place among built wonders.

Once from a bus window going into some city, Allahabad comes to mind, I saw a small white mosque in a green formal garden that looked like the Taj Mahal, evidently a replica. I went back to study this mosque. Indeed, it was a scale model with marble from the same quarry, every detail an exact copy. Yet what struck me was that despite this replica being physically the same in every detail, it was so clearly not the same as its archetype at all.

The great Taj Mahal is such an exquisite gem of architecture and this second mosque was so like it. Yet they were so different: the replica a lifeless building, pretty but not worth a second glance. Whereas the genuine Taj so struck me that my throat had a peculiar sensation.

I could not tell you with certainty what made the great difference between the bona fide treasure and the copy. No one could ever mistake one for the other. Due to advances in technology, modern replicas can be built with a fraction of the human labor that was necessary to build the original in the seventeenth century. That knowledge more than any physically visible difference must have been a factor in my judgment.

I could have gazed for days at the Taj and still not incorporate its dazzling white yet not-white exquisiteness. The white marble sparkling in the sunshine gave off scintillating glints of dazzling minute color amid the pure whiteness.

This replica was not the Taj by any stretch, but I was still glad to see it because it made me appreciate the real pearl of great price even more.

Sometimes even experts have difficulty distinguishing great works of art from forgeries. This replica did not appear to be an attempt at forgery, just an honest attempt at imitation. Does any reproduction, produced in the original medium as here in marble or by description with words or paint or clay, ever truly replicate the original? I think not.

Perhaps this is the foundation of the Islamic prohibition of graven images: that they realize the futility of attempting to capture real essence by some approximation of physical form.

With no paintings adorning the Taj Mahal, its architect believed that he was following the strict Muslim prohibition against images of God, human beings, or animals for worship. But was his very creation an imaging of God, Allah, Divinity?

The Shah Jehan, fifth ruler of the Mughal Empire in northern India, commissioned the Taj Mahal as tomb-mosque for his favorite wife, Mumtaz

Mahal, who died giving birth to their fourteenth child. The Shah spent the next two decades and depleted much of the royal treasury building this monument to their love. Thus, there might be other imagery of Divinity with it, too, in the respect that human sexual love as well as other sorts of human love are forms of communion between human beings and the Divine.

The Taj Mahal is the greatest, to me, of the great built wonders of the world, and the only one by which I was so entranced that I retraced my steps halfway across India to return for a second view under the light of the full moon. The experience was well worth my effort, but I think that I liked better the bright sun shining on the brilliant white marble to reflect glints of color.

What, or who, is Divine, God, Divinity? Humankind seems to have attempted to image the Divine as long as humankind has been in existence. With such a wide range of images, I am sure than no one artist has "it." On the other hand, I am oh, so glad that we keep trying because the results create invaluable treasures such as the Taj Mahal! I am so grateful that I was able to see it for myself. I ponder how I can repay somehow for the rare privilege. Is my writing this memoir recompense? I do not know, but I do know that humankind is so much the richer for this wonderful jewel.

ನ೨ೇ

Choosing second place on my list took no real decision making. Duomo of Milan, Italy, more or less decided for itself and like Iguaçu and Pamulkale, my finding it at all was pure serendipity.

I had wanted to get to Milan to catch an opera at La Scala before it closed for the season, so I ruthlessly cut short my time in the Swiss Alps in favor of the opera. In Milan I checked in at the hostel and then went for La Scala, hoping I was not too late. I was—its last performance of the season was the night before I arrived—some things in life we are too late to catch!

As I hurried along a small street toward La Scala, the street opened to a large plaza: there before me in the bright, full moon was the Duomo of Milan. Rarely had I seen anything so grand before or since!

Needing to hurry to La Scala, I could not dally then but knew that my very next priority after checking for tickets would be to return to gaze at that magnificent cathedral. A few minutes later, my disappointment at missing the opera was eased by joy in finding that frothy, gorgeous stone lacework in the bright moonlight.

I toyed with the idea of just staying there, leaning against a building across the plaza to admire Duomo in the moonlight all night long. From that vantage point, the moon appeared to move behind the structure, so I soon left for sleep. The next day, I returned to drink it in all day, including the interior.

The colossal stone building must have been very heavy yet appeared airy, fragile, and light as if someone, if giant enough, could pick it up and feel no weight at all. I was delighted by the many spires compared with only one found on many churches. Among these, one stood out as taller and more ornate.

Usually I do not find ornate tracery attractive to my aesthetic sense but I found this use of the style unique. Not one cubic inch was plain. Every inch was adorned yet the effect was never cloyingly "busy," more like an elaborate embroidery in stone.

I liked the exterior even more than the interior and found the entire cathedral marvelously pleasing, not Gothic, not Romanesque, or Byzantine, but in a class by itself.

Later I looked up a description of the architecture. The article classified it as "Northern European Gothic." Based on that, I had to revise my thought of "not Gothic," but it still looked different to me. The article also mentioned that the design outraged purist architects but delighted visitors. Obviously, I must be among the second group and am glad not to among the first.

The architects that find Duomo displeasing might be inclined more, as I was before this, toward unadorned simplicity.

ॐ

Number three on the list of built wonders, the New York City Chelsea Pumping Station, is of strictly utilitarian value. Deep underground, tourists rarely see it except by special arrangement. Beauty was not a consideration in its design.

I knew that the New York City water system transfers water from the Catskill/Delaware Mountain watershed, stores it in reservoirs, and brings it to the Hudson watershed by aqueducts, huge tunnels underground, into the city. But I did not realize, and think few people do, unless they are engineers or workers for the system, how great a great wonder it is after the water is brought to the outskirts of the city and then pumped to every apartment or office in the city, sometimes even higher than one thousand feet to be available by the flick of the wrist on a faucet tap.

I heard about a field trip to the pumping station for some New York City teachers and managed to secure an invitation to go along. After donning hard hats, we took an elevator down for what felt like a thousand feet but likely not. We learned that the level of the station was below the subway tunnels and the tunnels for gas and electricity; I am not sure about the sewer tunnels. I suppose in bedrock granite tunnels their relative positions do not matter; the contents of one would not commingle with the contents of another.

We stood on the catwalk spellbound by the huge machinery that pumped water to substations throughout the city, from where it is pumped to water mains serving neighborhoods, with further pumping mechanisms to get it up the tenth floor or even 110th floor.

Such mind-boggling achievement! I think no one but an engineer could fully appreciate this—and similar—constructions. To think that human beings could employ such genius and go to such great lengths to satisfy the human need to obtain (relatively) pure, healthy drinking water conveniently.

Our guide tried to explain the huge machinery that we were seeing. Admittedly, some of what he said was over my head, but I was able to glean a better understanding and appreciation for what is involved in coordinating the machinery of the system.

We were invited to walk single-file for a ways along the catwalk that was many miles long, with many branch-offs. Security did not appear to be a problem because it was not likely anyone other than authorized personnel could get through the locked steel doors or operate the elevator without security clearance.

In my inimitable way, though, I had to stop myself from wondering what if the authorized personnel or security staff was corrupt or went insane? I felt intimidated also to realize that even if a flashlight might light the darkness, there would be no escaping in the event of a power failure. Our guide reassured us that like hospitals and other essential service locations, the pumping system was equipped with a system for automatic shunting to emergency generators in case of power failure and there were big gates to shut off sections as necessary.

These contingencies must have been crucial when terrorist attacks on the World Trade Center collapsed buildings and subway tunnels. Officials must have been concerned that the devastation might have reached the water supply far beyond that black hole into which we peered. That none of these potentialities occurred seems to me to be some evidence that as well as the machinery being huge and complex, the designers must also have built in effective security components.

But awesome as that engineering feat was to me, it did not awe me as much as the sociopolitical engineering that built it. We had to summon the collective will to pay the billions of tax dollars to finance the project. As with all massive projects, this one required harnessing of many workers over many years to dig the tunnels, lay the pipe, build the system, and now to maintain the system. As technology improves, the system has continually been upgraded; now computers regulate the flow.

None of those many workers was a slave either, although possibly figuratively we might all envision ourselves as slaves if we want to look at it that way. We are "slaves" to the need to work to pay for food, shelter, and clothing for our dependents and ourselves. These workers enjoyed as much "free choice" about their choice of livelihood as is available in this world though.

No doubt the workers building the Duomo of Milan had some choice over what job they opted to take also, and in their case, their work might have been buoyed by an inner sense that their work was, in addition to being a livelihood, also serving their God. Egyptian workers on the pyramids might have had similar choice inspired by comparable beliefs about their pharaoh, whom they believed *was* their God, was he not? The Hebrews at that time though were slaves.

I wondered whether the pumping-station builders might have been buoyed up in the face of their daily grind by the knowledge that they were serving their fellow human beings, that their toil was useful labor.

I found the democracy embodied in the pumping-station project as beautiful as I found the physical aspects of the pumping station aesthetically unbeautiful. By comparison, Shah Jehan wanted a beautiful memorial for his favorite wife, had the power to order it done, and did, with no democratic process needed. But in New York City, to secure a water supply for the city, to move beyond digging wells for each individual household, the people exercised communal decision making to formulate plans, execute the plans, and live with the consequences of their actions. The energy came from the people in their own interest instead of being foisted on them on the whim of a dictator. In that way, I saw representative democracy as the builder of this great modern wonder.

࿇

When I was in Greece the first time, I so regretted missing the Parthenon that I made seeing it a high priority on my second visit. I found it marvelous beyond description, though by this very listing I have ranked it comparable to other built wonders and not on par with the Taj Mahal. I think possibly one reason the Taj and Duomo of Milan edged it out is that when I visited those sites, I was alone and could let the wonder wash over me, whereas I saw the Parthenon on a guided tour. We pay for these tours as though they enhance the experience, but for me a regulated itinerary diminishes my enjoyment of a place. Nonetheless, if the site is truly a wonder, the presence of a tour group and guide cannot eliminate its essence such that its identity is lost.

The Parthenon was so remarkable in my estimation that I wondered why it did not make the list of the ancient "seven wonders of the world," all gone now without a trace except for the Great Pyramid of Egypt. Granted, the Great Pyramid is a wondrous site, but to me not remarkable enough to rank on my list of "top seven."

The Parthenon appears to celebrate the creation of humankind. The frieze depicts the Council of the Gods in the course of debating whether the creation of humankind was good. Originally, at the entrance of the Parthenon stood the splendid statue of Athena, goddess with whom the god Hephaestus created the first woman, made of gold and ivory. She stood upon a podium decorated with a frieze celebrating the birth of the first human woman through whom humankind was licensed to multiply and populate the Earth.

Since the "ancient" Greeks and Romans devised the original list of "Seven Wonders of the Ancient World," perhaps they viewed the Parthenon as their "modern" marvel, not even in contention for the original list. For the fifth century BCE, what a modern marvel it was.

Although straight lines appear to prevail in the architectural form of the Parthenon, there is actually not one single straight line in it. The pedestal bases are curvilinear. Marvelous optical rules were devised to ensure that the Parthenon's corner columns are slightly larger in diameter than the others. This was done because the more well-lighted an object is, the less voluminous it appears. By widening the corner columns that catch the most light, all the columns appear to be of the same thickness. What is even more amazing is that the ancient architects knew exactly how much thicker a corner column should be and how much closer it needed to be placed to the adjacent column than the distance between each of the other columns to achieve this effect. The architects of the Parthenon avoided straight lines because there are no straight lines in nature. By not having any, therefore, the temple blended more harmoniously into its surroundings.

I think that I recognize a reason that I was so moved by the Parthenon. I am a product of the heritage of Western civilization: its history and culture. For that grand heritage, the Parthenon epitomizes the standard of simple classical beauty. Heir to that culture, I have its standards deeply ingrained in me without any element of choice on my part.

There was a feature of the Parthenon that just a trifle disturbed me. I knew that the British had removed a large portion of the frieze and the original columns from Greece and that they are on display as the Elgin Marbles in a British museum. Greece contends that Lord Elgin, British ambassador to the Ottoman Empire, stole these artifacts in 1801. Britain contends that Lord Elgin had permission from the ruling Turkish authorities to take them. Greece has been demanding the return of the Elgin Marbles since the country's independence from Turkey in 1829. That debate is ongoing.

Meanwhile, the columns on display at the site of the original Parthenon are mostly replicas. I am glad that the Greeks have been doing restoration of the site, even though I would be just as fascinated if there were no columns left to see there at all. But the ethical dilemma I sensed in the viewing was that I could not, as I had at the Taj Mahal copy, distinguish the difference between these replicas and the originals.

What made the difference of seeing the one as copy but unable to see the other as copy? I do not think it was merely that world-class experts had done the Parthenon reconstruction.

As I stared at the wonder of the Parthenon, I was so very grateful that the ancient Greeks, with all their faults of slavery and subjugation of women and civil warring and other deficiencies (which people in history had no flaws?) left this wonderful heritage of "The Beautiful," not just in the architecture that so enthralled me on the spot, but in their tradition of architecture, art, sculpture, drama, poetry, history writing, and philosophy. With the gratitude for that rich, rich heritage was also something akin to shame that I was so ignorant of most of it and I resolved to begin correcting my deficiency on return by reading some of the plays and Greek authors.

I did follow through with that resolve. In that sense, the Parthenon might even rank higher than the first three in that it had a more positive influence on my later reading habits. I did not know of a vast rich heritage of common knowledge that would correspond to the Taj or the Duomo as Greek literature did to the Parthenon and it was a benefit that so much of the great Greek literature was available in English translation, but gradually my interests did expand to Renaissance literature, too. Of course, for such spin-off delights even twenty lifetimes would be too short to savor them all.

户♥

As with great natural wonders, after the first few deciding on a rank ordering becomes increasingly difficult, but the Hindu-Buddhist carvings in the living rock of Ellora and Ajanta caves not far from Aurangabad, India, rank high on any list. I discovered the caves while reading tourist literature at the Indian Embassy in Moscow when I was "hiding out" from the Intourist officials. I visited Ellora on one day and Ajanta on the next.

These caves are not remarkable for their character as caves per se, but for the temple carvings in the solid rock on the walls. In fact, the caves themselves appear not to be naturally occurring, but instead seem to have been carved out of the solid rock face of the cliffs that existed there before. In all, there are thirty-four caves at Ellora: twelve Buddhist, seventeen Hindu, and five Jain. The Hindu Caves are the most dramatic of the Ellora cave temples. Unlike the Ellora caves, Ajanta Caves are all Buddhist. These caves are famous for their magnificent paintings. Five of the caves are *chaitaya*s or temples, while the other twenty-four are *viharas* or monasteries.

The caves I toured were quite shallow. I quickly lost the sense of being in a cave. The feeling was more like a city of temples and carvings. Since my standards of beauty run along the lines of the Parthenon or the Taj Mahal, I cannot say that I found these elaborate carvings "beautiful." Neither did I sense a tremendous power in them as I had felt when viewing the Chelsea Pumping Station in New York City.

What impressed me was the thought of the hundreds (working a few at a time as the space permitted) of Hindu, Jain, and Buddhist monk stonework artists who created these incredible works of art that I recognized *as* art, though I had not the sensibilities to appreciate it as it deserved to be appreciated.

Although I was too unfamiliar with the Jain, Hindu, and Buddhist religions to understand *why*, I did very well understand *that* these carvings had a deep religious and aesthetic significance to some people of those faiths.

I realized then how much of the awe I felt at seeing some of our Western-heritage art and architecture such as the Gothic cathedrals was owing to my prior understanding of the religious and cultural heritage associated with what I was seeing. Even without that background knowledge, I could marvel at the enormous work and skill these cave sculptures represented.

In the case of the Taj Mahal, many workers under the direction of a single designer executed his vision. In the case of Ellora and Ajanta, there was a collective design that evolved literally over centuries.

The mystery of how Ellora and Ajanta were carved—I could not imagine just how the magnificent temple building had been done—added to their wonder. These structures were not "built" as most temple buildings are constructed by putting stones on top of one another, according to a blueprint.

I have seen articles with diagrams of how huge stones could be placed according to a "blueprint" by rollers, ropes, trenches, and mounds later removed or how huge stones such as those of Stonehenge and the pyramids could be put on top of one another. These diagrams allowed me to get a dim picture in my mind of how it may have been accomplished.

For Ellora and Ajanta, there was no such stone placing but the opposite, removing unwanted stone. The artisans sculpted in reverse, so to speak; not taking a block and chiseling off until the form they had in mind remained, but taking a rock wall and chiseling it away until a sort of building remained, full of further carvings of gods and beings or designs. The resulting edifice is entirely carved from one solid piece of stone.

I was reminded of the great four heads on Mount Rushmore also carved, somehow, from a rock wall. I do marvel at those. In that case, there was a single designer to direct the work but many workers aided by machinery to execute the plan. In the case of Mount Rushmore, the loss of the mountainside's natural wonder in favor of a built wonder troubled me.

The caves did not strike me as the same sort of loss, since I did not view caves as natural wonders destroyed for the sake of a built wonder. More like I viewed the pumping station, I viewed this as underground stone that we might never see at all if not for the enhancement done by human beings. So I did not see this sort of building as detrimental unless, of course, as is often the case, workers lost life or limb in the process.

The commissioners of such great wonders also capture my fascination. Hindu, Jain, and Buddhist religious leaders must have commissioned Ellora and Ajanta. Even if they had the cooperation or endorsement of the civil rulers—not Shahs of Mogul regimes because they would never sanction carving images—they would not have needed any input from the masses.

I guessed that religious motives more than civil causes motivated these works because devotees of these religions believe in incarnation. They hold that doing good works in this life is meritorious and that accumulating merit during this life will afford better status and more abundance—power, wealth, beauty, and health—in the next.

We know the pharaohs used absolute civil political power commissioned the building of their tombs—pyramids—even though the structures played a role in their worship and religious beliefs. We also have written records to give us glimpses into the commissioning of other built wonders and this sort of information about the carvings in Ellora and Ajanta may be available, too, but I did not get it. My life seemed too short then, and is too short now, to hunt for it. I am content to conjecture about the answers to my questions.

On a practical level, I wondered what they did with the stone chips left over from carving. Did they carry them out in baskets? How did they do that when some of the stones must have been huge? Such mysteries continue to fuel my curiosity and wonder after nearly half a century.

૭≈ఆ

Seeing Stonehenge was one of my major objectives in going to England. We think that its commissioners were the Druids. I do not know if I saw it at the best of times or the worst of times. I arrived around the first of March 1956, mid-winter, before the World Heritage project to restore the site in the mid-1980s. Now they have replaced those huge, *huge* stone lintels atop their uprights and rearranged them into a huge, *huge* circle, as originally built. That has helped so that visitors can see with their eyes instead of having to do the harder task of mental imaging. I think I might have preferred such restoration.

At that time though, despite the heap of huge slabs rather jumbled around, enough of them were still upright and in a pattern that I could discern as circular. I was lucky in having seen diagrams of it before I went so in imagination I could see it as must have been, at least some.

A delightful plus for me was that I managed to be alone amid those massive stones. Now I understand there are always crowds of tourists there.

For me, solitude improves imagining.

Sometimes a guide is helpful in pointing out details that I might otherwise have missed. More often the guide is droning on about something all but irrelevant to me, interrupting my contemplation of some other more captivating aspect of the wonder. Likewise, crowds tend to distract me.

The listmakers who devised the "Seven Wonders of the Ancient World" must never have traveled far enough away from Greece or Rome to see Stonehenge, or they would most certainly have awarded it a place on the list. If they had, I could not fathom which of the seven would have had to be deleted to make room for it.

I pondered the Druid priests who had the religious—and whatever political—power to harness the human energy of thousands of workers necessary to move these colossal stones, a wonder not as much for their beauty but for the amount of human power harnessed and the ingenuity of its engineering some four or five millennia ago, before even the Pyramids of Egypt were built.

Could it be that the Druids had already noticed the same astronomical periodicity and "music of the spheres" conjectured by Pythagoras, Plato, and Johannes Kepler? Did they commission Stonehenge as an observatory for scientific study of the skies? Or did they perform religious or pagan rituals there, perhaps human sacrifice?

I was baffled by the thought that these ancient sun worshippers could have been wise enough to recognize the revolution of Earth around the sun each year and built this megalithic altar to align directly with the rising of the sun upon sunrise of the summer solstice—but not to recognize the inhumanity and indecency of human sacrifice!

For what purpose this human sacrifice?—to appease some weird god notion? I was not familiar with Druid notions about that and meant to study Druidism some, but I never have. I did have a hazy notion that in Druid mystic beliefs the universe itself was the deity's temple, so they may not have needed temples made with the hands.

The notion of an open-air temple appealed to me. I mused about the scene if the summer solstice fell on a rainy day so that the alignment of stones and sun could not be visually observed, so that a sacrificial fire could not be lit, the sacrifice not burned, the devotees getting thoroughly drenched!

The day I was there was sunny. I thought about the effect rain, mist, and fog might have had on the building. Would mud-slick terrain make transporting the stones easier, or would rain have delayed operations?

The thought of all the potential obstacles that confronted the ancient Celts and their Druid priests juxtaposed with their exceptional achievement staggers me.

❧

Rank ordering the "top seven" after number one really makes no sense to me—deciding which ones make the list and which fall short—since they all "tie" in my estimation. With that said, I arbitrarily filled the last spot with Machu Picchu along the Inca Trail in modern Peru. I celebrated the three-day Fourth of July weekend that year with an excursion to Machu Picchu ("Old Mountain").

After a train ride up on the first morning, I hiked the remaining way up a steep path to the city. The third day was filled with the hike and train ride back down to Cuzco. That left me with more time to absorb the experience than I had with most of the other built wonders. I would have loved more time at each site and repeat trips to them as well, but we all have to accommodate the reality of having only one lifetime to experience our world.

That extra time might play a role in why I rated the experience so high. Had I but five minutes there, I still would have been struck speechless.

This "Lost City of the Incas" lay undiscovered for hundreds of years after the last of the Incas left until Hiram Bingham rediscovered it in 1911. The city is intact except for straw roofs that have rotted away. The site is a maze of plazas and palaces, long staircases carved out of the solid rock, and terraces that go right to the edge of sheer cliffs.

In any setting Machu Picchu would not be less a wonder, but its magnificent setting in the Urubamba Gorge amid emerald—not snowcapped there—peaks of the Andes towering above adds to the splendor.

Like Stonehenge, Machu Picchu contains an observatory among its many buildings that incorporate characteristic trapezoidal doorways. The Intihuatana stone ("Hitching Post of the Sun") has been shown to be a precise indicator of the date of the two equinoxes and other significant celestial periods. At midday on 21 March and 21 September, the sun stands almost directly above the pillar, creating no shadow at all. At this precise moment, the sun "sits with all his might upon the pillar" and is for a moment "tied" to the rock.

The Incan empire based its religion on a cult of the Sun. While the winter solstice is on 21 June in the southern hemisphere, the Pacha Unachaq, a sundial used by the Incas, indicated that the sun stays some days in the same place before rising on 24 June. Therefore, an Incan high priest declared 24 June to be the New Year. The moment that the sun touches the Intihuatana on 24 June each year, the Inti Raymi, the Festival of the Sun, is celebrated.

It just amazes me how those ancients without what we consider basic tools of communication, such as writing, were nevertheless able to fathom the wonderful periodicity of the solar system. In modernity we have the technology to send out space probes and even walk on the moon. Those ancients traveled outer space in their minds so to speak.

Some of the North American pre-Columbian peoples also knew of this periodicity. Cahokia Mounds near East St. Louis has a sort of observatory that sights on the summer solstice at sunrise.

I could write volumes more about Machu Piccu, but with oceans of words I would not be able convey the wonder. Instead, I can only invite you to "see for yourself." If that option is not open to you, then you can just let your imagination carry you to that Incan city among the Andean peaks with the many photos and articles that feature it found in any library.

❧

So there you have my "top seven" built wonders of the world as I saw them during my travels. As I cautioned you though, to stop at seven would shortchange the many other human-built wonders and human events that fill my memories.

Pre-Aztec Teotihuacan, Mexico, that arose as a new religious center around the time of Christ, is not far from Mexico Distrito Federal.

By the time I saw Teotihuacan, I had seen Stonehenge, the pyramids of Egypt, and the Buddhist city of Pagan, with its over 2,000 temples, pagodas, stupas, and shrines. I do not know if my experience of them affected my feeling that Teotihuacan was a lesser wonder. I still admired the big, dead city, with its long central avenue with the colossal Pyramid of the Sun at one end and the slightly less colossal yet majestic Pyramid of the Moon at the other. These reminded me of the Pyramids of Egypt enough to start me fantasizing (theorizing?) that perhaps pre-Columbian peoples had contact with the builders of the Egyptian pyramids and had copied their work.

Could sailing ships have blown off course? Egyptians relied on Phoenicians for such sailing though, true? I decided that copying probably was not a factor. Even young children building with blocks are likely to come up with pyramid structures. So these pre-Aztec people may have built their big pyramids solely from their own imaginings or that of the tiny elite priesthood. But it seems very likely the later Mayans and Aztecs copied *them*, both in pyramid and temple construction as well as gruesomely in human sacrifice.

As at Stonehenge, I was alone at Teotihuacan. My imagination could roam. I envisioned myself climbing the steep high steps as a priest ready to meet the god in the shrine at the top and later drag the sacrifice out to roll down those steep steps to the crowd below. I shuddered.

Then I saw myself the sacrifice, captured in a raid, victim to the priests, and shuddered more.

∾∾

Taking a big jump to the East, my thoughts turn to the Buddhist pagodas of Pagan in Myanmar. The pagodas were another of the rare sites of which I had never heard before arriving in the region. I cannot recall whether I learned of them while I was at the Moulmein pagoda or on the boat steaming down the Irrawaddy. But I did hear of it in time to catch the experience by getting off the steamer, later to continue my journey down the river. So I did.

Asking the boat officer to pull over so that I could disembark was easy. Thinking about standing on the shore waving to a boat in midstream hoping that it would pull over to pick me up again made me uneasy. I wondered whether they could even see me standing there from so far away. Ever the optimist, I figured if they missed me on my first attempt that would allow me another day to experience the marvel. As a last resort, I guessed that I could make my way overland to catch a bus.

I disembarked at what seemed to be the middle of the jungle. There was a broad path leading up the bank and off into that jungle, so I took it.

After some less than a quarter of a mile as I rounded a bend—or went over a hill, I cannot now really say—I nearly fainted in joyful shock.

My breath left me for several moments as I surveyed—not 10,000 of William Wordsworth's golden daffodils tossing their heads in spritely dance *alive*, but 10,000 (?) pagoda almost-ruins there on the hillside.

These were off-white, not shiny white, but streaked with the gray of age and ruin. A cynic might have said, "dirty white." Certainly these were not the dazzling white of the Taj Mahal. Still the people who had told me I must not leave Myanmar without seeing the pagodas did not overrate the sight. I think that overrating Pagan is impossible. Yes, it almost made my "top seven" and probably tied for some of those. Yet, as nearly always in the presence of such greatness, words fail me. To be more precise, I think that the words fail not only me, but just fail. Period.

Wordsworth described the 10,000 daffodils he saw at a glance. I wished he had seen these 10,000 pagodas at a glance as I did. Maybe he could have come up with a description that would have done them justice.

Rather than beauty or power, perhaps their impact lies in how they represent humankind striving for Divinity? Yet the Buddha shunned any consideration of whatever Divinity is by stressing that a person can find enlightenment-salvation by following the eight-fold path. Thus, I did not think that the pagoda builders were striving to please a deity.

So what was the great attraction of this hillside full of pagodas ruins? Despite the ravishes of time, they were still unmistakably recognizable as pagodas or stupas. I never did get the distinction between pagoda and stupa.

Some, maybe all, represent Buddha: The square base his cloak, the rounded dome-like part his "begging" bowl. Other features of the stupa-pagodas also symbolize parts of Buddha, but I have forgotten in what ways.

I was also astonished at the deadness of these pagodas when all over Myanmar other pagodas are *alive* with people coming to—worship without belief in a deity might be the wrong word—renew their resolve to follow the eight-fold way more nearly.

The liveliness of Burmese pagodas was in a way reminiscent of Wordsworth's daffodils in spritely dance—the pagoda bodhi-leaf wind bells did dance spritely. The sun shining makes them appear golden, better than daffodils, since they also make such pleasing music to captivate our hearing as well as our sight. Sometimes still I still hear the tinkling music of Mayanmar's pagoda bells in my mind's ears. The music brings bliss to my solitude.

The pagodas of Pagan were silent. I missed the sound of the bells.

Why were all these pagodas dead anyhow? I surmised and later found my guess corroborated by a bit of reading that while the reasons for Pagan's abandonment are not known with any certainty, political rulers built the pagodas from respect for their Buddhist religion, but the occupants may have fled when faced with the armies of Kublai Khan. For centuries after, it stood derelict, with its treasures plundered. People believed that it became the hideout for bandits and Nats, the amoral spirits of Buddhist beliefs.

I thought about relations between church and state, or pagoda and state. I was glad that the rebels against church-state from England wrote out the principle that in our country we would respect separation of church and state, even as I recognized that in some cultures that I had seen the culture was so permeated with customs from religion that no separation was easily distinguished. I intended to study relations of culture, religion, and state later, and I did, a little.

In that way, traveling can become frustrating. The more I saw, the more I saw so much more to see and to study. Giving way to that frustration could lead to a sort of despair that anything worth learning cannot ever be learned and result in never getting a start. But to me any amount of travel, even if it just scratches the surface of all the possibilities, is such a joy!

I slept among the pagodas of Pagan that night, glad for my habit of carrying food and water for just this kind of contingency.

Next morning I reluctantly returned to the river to flag down a boat. One picked me up shortly, so my unease about that had been unwarranted.

The Wat at Angkor, Cambodia, is surrounded by many other shrines and temples. Angkor Wat gives its name to the whole mighty complex. These are not only Buddhist, but also Hindu. The two traditions are closely related.

This sort of syncretism is difficult to understand by those reared in "no other gods before—or beside—me" and "Christ is the only—the whole, the absolute—way, the truth, and the life" traditions. But it works for Hindus and Buddhists to mix and yet remain unmixed, as inconsistent as that sounds. So the monuments of Angkor are full of carvings of Hindu deities and epics as well as statues of the Buddha. Besides these, some of the carvings are secular.

Of course, I had not enough knowledge of their culture to half appreciate this Angkor Wat, but I was dumbfounded at so *much* human accomplishment there in the jungle where modern civilization is slowly—would be rapidly without efforts to stay the encroachment as much as possible, except in a few places to show the power of the jungle—crumbling these magnificent ruins.

Besides the majesty and grandeur, I learned that this temple is a representation in stone of the mythological Mount Meru, the center or navel of the universe, abode of the gods, in both Hindu and Buddhist cosmology. The five towers of the lofty temple represent the five peaks of Mount Meru.

The steps up each level are very steep. I climbed past each of the five terraces to the topmost level, with its shrine, the central tower or peak, the other four being at the four cardinal points. All the many other buildings seemed to be situated on a square base representing the four cardinal points. Friezes were all around each level, with carvings of bulbous-breasted goddesses, gods, demons, and stories in stone carvings of Hindu epics.

I noticed that despite the many carvings of gods, there were no statues, as I had seen in some temples, of the Buddha. Nor did I notice one of the favorite Hindu gods, elephant-headed Ganesh. He might have been there, I do not recall.

At the pinnacle, I had a great view of the perimeter wall, which represents the wall of mountains surrounding *the* Mountain, and the square pools on either side of the causeway, which represent the cosmic ocean out of which the universe was churned. Even the thought of climbing was exhilarating. Such mountains have to be climbed!

Climbing, reaching the top of this stone symbol of a mountain was as exhilarative if not more so even than when I had climbed natural mountains.

இ~௭

Another site that really impressed me was Dome of the Rock in Old City, Jerusalem. Not long after the Muslims captured Jerusalem in the seventh century, their leader commissioned the Dome. The site chosen, Mount Moriah, was the very same rock where previously had been two temples of the Jews, the first built during the reign of Solomon to house the Ark of the Covenant. Nebuchadrezzar II of Babylon destroyed that after he forced the Jews into exile. After Cyrus of Persia conquered Babylon, he allowed the Jews to return to Jerusalem and they rebuilt the temple but without the Ark.

After the Roman general Pompey captured Jerusalem, he enlarged the second temple and added the famous Western Wall. The Romans finally razed the temple. Roman emperor Hadrian commissioned a temple to the god Jove (the Greek god Jupiter) erected on the same spot and when the area became Christian, it was left as a symbol of Christian triumphalism.

Did the Muslims also choose the site to demonstrate triumphalism and suppression of both Christianity and Judaism? Was their intention to evince the power of the Sultan who commissioned it? Was it a sign of sincere worship of Allah the Beneficent One in stone?

There is some religious significance to this mount that crosses both the Islamic and the Judaic tradition. Both the Qu'ran and the Torah tell the story of the patriarch Ibrahim (Abraham) who was asked by God (Allah) to sacrifice his son Ismail (as incorporated later into the Old Testament, the name of the son was said to be Isaac). The region of Moriah is where the sacrifice was prepared.

The Muslims also believe that a passage in the Qu'ran links the Prophet Mohammed and Mecca with Jerusalem and the Temple Mount. Mohammed, accompanied by the Archangel Gabriel, journeyed to Jerusalem from Mecca. After stopping briefly on Mount Sinai and in Bethlehem, Israel, they arrived on Mount Moriah, where they encountered Abraham, Moses, Jesus, and other prophets, whom Mohammed led in prayer. Gabriel then escorted Mohammed to the pinnacle of the rock where a ladder of golden light materialized. On the ladder Mohammed ascended through the seven heavens into the presence of

Allah, from whom he received instructions for himself and his followers. Following the divine meeting, he was flown back to Mecca by Gabriel on a winged horse.

The dome is not a mosque, but a mashhad, or shrine, for pilgrims and while built by Muslims, its architecture is unique to the Muslim world—very much like the Roman architecture seen in the Cathedral of Bosra in Persia. Covered with blue tile below, a golden dome twenty meters high and ten meters in diameter sits atop it. The original covering of real gold was removed over the centuries and was replaced with anodized aluminum. With the sun shining on it, it was bright golden enough for me—like life itself, mostly. Of course, there are cloudy times that make life a bit gray at times.

Sixteen arches that came from different churches in Jerusalem destroyed during the Persian occupation encircle the foundation stone on the interior. Worship included circling the sacred foundation stone seven-times under the dome. The stone is a huge boulder with a hole drilled in it.

I wondered how the builders had precision tools so many centuries ago for drilling such a hole. I had never heard any Jewish claims about the rock or the hole being sacred to them, not like the Western Wall, the only remains of their former temple. But tourist blurbs explained the hole was there to carry off the blood of the lambs sacrificed daily to God in the temple before the Romans destroyed it. That made me wonder whether that destruction, such a horrific blow to the Jews at the time, in the long turning of the years did not turn out after all as a blessing in disguise that forced a change in forms of worship from animal sacrifice to "deeds of loving kindness."

I could not decide whether I found the Dome of the Rock such a built wonder from its artful architecture, though there is certainly that, especially in its use of geometric ratios some few of which I caught, or in the religious-cultural associations for me both as the previous Temple of Judaism and because Mount Moriah is so close to the Mount of Olives where Jesus Christ is said to have ascended into Heaven.

இ~௯

In 1982 on my second trip to Jerusalem was to wade through Hezekiah's Tunnel.

In ancient Jerusalem at the time of Hezekiah, King of the Israelites, Assyrians were laying siege on the city. Not wanting them to find plenty of water there, Hezekiah blocked the upper outlet of the Gihon spring and channeled the water down to the west side of the City of David. Hezekiah had this third-of-a-mile-long tunnel carved through stone to bring water from one side of the city to the other, under ground.

So Hezekiah's Tunnel was not to serve Yahweh per se, but dug in preparation for war, for survival as then seen necessary to cope with the exigencies of the day, not for noble notions of justice, right, abundance, and love for a humankind of which there are no more enemies because the attitudes and actions of enmity have dissolved in a long, slow ascent to a higher level of human decency. Yet I mused, if not excused, that after all, for humanity to grow, first humanity must survive.

The tunnel is considered the greatest marvels of water engineering technology of the pre-Classical period. Depending on rainfall, the tunnel can be quite full of water and depending on how tall the traveler, as high as chest deep. The wading takes considerable effort as the current is quite strong. But I waded knee deep the whole length of the tunnel. It was a thrill to last my lifetime and Hezekiah's Tunnel has lasted many lifetimes—some twenty-four centuries.

I find it odd that amid all my thrill at wading through it, not until this writing about it some thirty years after the fact did I wonder whether it still serves as a water supply for the City of Jerusalem. I believe it does, but channeled after the tunnel itself for use in modern taps. I am not sure about that.

∾∾

I have found some of the still-existing architectural structures of some of our indigenous peoples quite fascinating. Many earthen mounds remain, both archaeological ruins and restorations.

I found Canyon de Chelly (pronounced can-yon duh-shay) in Arizona to be one of my favorites. I love the delightful cottonwood grove at its mouth and its aspect as a canyon. This Navajo land, the longest continuously inhabited landscape of North America, has distinctive architecture, artifacts, and rock imagery, and the land sustains a living community of Navajo people who are connected by their collective memory to a landscape of great historical and spiritual significance.

In a peculiar way I liked this canyon even better than Grand Canyon. Grand Canyon is *so* grand that falls beyond human scale, so awesome that it seemed more for gods than humans. But Canyon de Chelly is on a human scale: I could "get" it, so to speak, whereas Grand Canyon is so mighty maybe nobody can "get" it all. For those reasons, I almost put Canyon de Chelly as a natural wonder, human sized, instead of a built wonder. But it is a joint Navajo and United States National Monument, entirely located on Navajo land, for its cliff dwellings akin to those of Mesa Verde more than any special natural grandeur, though it had that for me. The cliff dwellings there, built into the canyon walls, are a value added wonder for the site.

I had a very childish delight at Canyon de Chelly, too. In the lovely cottonwood grove is a campsite of the usual national monument or park campsite standard, including showers. So I camped there as a delightful second home— my roofless, wall-less home.

Wall-less. I was intrigued by that impossible triple-"l" word that does not exist in the English language, so we have to stick in a hyphen to separate out the third letter. Now why should our language be so artificial? I was surprised I had to be in a community that existed before the English language was invented to discover that illogicality. But when I returned home I wondered why I had not noticed this aberration before—not until my wall-less campsite second home on the Navajo Reservation—because I walked right in to see that I have a beautiful view from my apartment window of a hill-line.

Memoirs can be silly as well as sublime!

But there in Canyon de Chelly, I realized the sublimity first of language and second of the invention of *writing* language. And without a doubt writing must be *the* greatest "built wonder" of the entire history of the human race.

Now *that* is awesome to me.

When I discovered the same sublimity of language in the tiny portion of it as "written English" in my own home, I thought that there is no need to travel at all to discover some of the greatest wonders.

So maybe no "need" but surely still "great reason" to travel: It shakes up a bit old, ingrained habits of thought or feeling or "culture" so that we can see in our own home phenomena that have always been present, but notice them, or see them in new ways that might never have occurred to us had we not left home at all. The amusing never-a-triple-"l" word rule is just a concrete example of other more important, albeit more subtle, discoveries waiting for us to notice.

৯৽৶

Generally, I feel so lucky that I had the means and the time to travel to such wonders for the pure human enjoyment all my experiences afforded me.

These are all my personal feelings and reactions to what I saw. "They say" travel is broadening, and I have certainly found my own travel to be so. More than broadening, I found it heightening and deepening, of my learning, understanding, feeling, and, I hope, wisdom, though I can never be sure about that. All around us are wonders to behold, abroad but even more at home, in everyday living, to anyone who has eyes or imagination to *see*. I do not suppose my ability to see or imagine is any more or better than anyone else's, but I felt an inner compulsion to write this memoir to share with others what I have seen.

STUDY QUESTIONS

1. In speaking about human sacrifice, probably involuntarily given by poor workers, possibly slaves, even loss of life, to build the wonders on her list she says, "Oh, it was *worth* the cost!"

- What does this exclamation imply about how the author values human life?

- Is this value consistent with other claims made by the author regarding our duty to oppressed peoples?

2. In describing the Taj Mahal and its replica, the author says, "I could not tell you with certainty what made the great difference between the bona fide treasure and the copy"
- Discuss some factors that might have contributed to the author's ability to distinguish these two edifices that she did not mention.

3. The author focuses a great deal on the Chelsea Pumping Station.
- What values of the author are suggested by her strong attraction to this site?
- Compare and contrast the author's thrill at the pumping station and other built wonders with her emotions experienced upon seeing natural wonders.

4. The author says that unlike the replica of the Taj Mahal, she could not tell the difference between the authentic Parthenon and the replica that had been built as a restoration. She asks, "What made the difference of seeing the one as copy but unable to see the other as copy?"
- How would you answer the author's question?

5. Claiming to travel to find solutions to problems of oppressed peoples, the author says, "As I stared at . . . the Parthenon I was . . . grateful that the ancient Greeks, with all their faults of slavery and subjection of women and civil warring and other deficiencies . . . left this wonderful heritage of 'The Beautiful'"
- Is this statement consistent with the author's stated values motivating her travel?
- Discuss the concept of situational ethics.

6. About creators of the built wonders, the author says, "love is the nearest I can come to describe some inner emotion that humans have inspiring them to do some work, great or small, beyond fear of physical punishment as consequence for avoiding the work."
- Do you agree with the author's assessment of what motivates human beings to build wondrous constructions?
- How does personal human love of one individual for another relate to the love that inspires someone to build physical structures?

Eight

OTHER ENCOUNTERS

I have forgotten more encounters that I have had than I remember. Of those I had that I remember, many would be better forgotten. Of the rest, some are worthy to be included in my memoirs.

One of the things I remember most vividly about India is the Shiva Linga. The first time I saw one, I stopped short, in shock. I must have a "dirty mind," for to me the object looked like an erect penis. No, my mind is "pure" enough. I learned that is exactly what a Shiva Linga represents!

Shiva, most-revered of Hindu gods, has many roles to play, among them is that he is the seed of life. Hindus worship the phallic symbol, representing Shiva's primeval creative energy in many temples. His principle consort, Parvati ("she who dwells in the mountains"), is represented by the *yoni*, Sanskrit word for vagina, loosely translated as "sacred space" or "Sacred Temple." Parvati fulfills and completes Shiva's creative tendencies. The image of the linga in the yoni is the most common image of the deity in Shiva temples. Though the name Shiva was connected with lingua, I never heard of the name Parvati being directly named with yoni.

Now if there is any deity in Hinduism that might be called promiscuous, that would be Lord Krishna, who is known for establishing courtship with 1,600 Gopinis or milkmaids of Brindaban, India, which I imagined as a sort of idyllic Forest of Arden where Krishna seduced with his magic flute.

I found it odd that with so many milkmaids with whom Krishna could sport, there did not seem to be any other men to complicate the sporting.

After my shock at first sighting the phallic symbols, I realized these were in no way pornographic. Instead, they serve as reminders of the power of generation of the human species and more as sermons in stone to guard and keep that power for its proper use.

It is one thing to see linga in all sizes all over India but quite another to be casually going through the Brooklyn Museum of Art and see a six-foot-tall linga in the middle of the gallery. From my experience in India, I recognized it, but went to check its identification plaque to be sure. It was, of course, but what surprised me was to see the linga presented as art or ethnography instead of as a religious representation in places of worship. To me it is not aesthetic. Then I recalled my thoughts about whether aesthetics and religious representations can be separated. Perhaps the same human impulse drives both creative impulses, to transcend the crass or mundane, possibly by depicting the mundane not as "crass" but as aesthetic or divine, looking for signs of the

Divinity in commonplace objects. Later I saw the linga in other museums as of art or ethnography.

In addition to the Shiva Linga ubiquitous in India, there are also many pictorial representations of Shiva. Shiva as Nataraja, Lord of the Cosmic Dance, is a common theme.

I am attracted to the notion of cosmic dance, for dance is *patterned* movement—thus representing the cosmos as having a pattern, not chaotic, not as a "formless void," but orderly, patterned, with an eternal circling of the solar system, galaxy, universe.

৯৵৻৶

There was an encounter on the streets of Calcutta that still brings a chuckle at the remembering. The way to buy anything after crossing the Hellespont from Europe into Asia and then to Africa, or on this side of the world crossing the Rio Grande heading south is to bargain. Bargaining is time consuming, but I quite enjoyed it unless I had something else pressing to do for I was there to take time to learn, enjoy, and use the customs of the country, and I became quite good at it.

A sidewalk vendor in Calcutta had strawberries so luscious looking that I just had to get some, and later a bottle of water to wash them. So I settled to quite a lengthy bargaining session and finally got one of the only two baskets he had left at what I considered a good price, though my conscience did trouble me as I thought I could have afforded more and he probably needed the money more than I did. Part of the process was not to give so much that his need would be obvious, the charity hurting his dignity, and not to give up too easily so that I, as the customer, appeared stupid.

This vendor appeared delighted that I had so shrewdly finally outplayed him at the fine game. We were both enjoying that post-buying time when an Indian woman approached. She indicated interest in the last remaining basket of strawberries, and the bargaining began again. He indicated a price far beyond what I had just paid and with his eyes implored me not to give him away. I smiled my complicity and watched the bargaining proceed with high amusement. She finally bought the strawberries at a price quite far above the one I paid. There I was, the foreigner, out-bargaining the native!

That exemplified one of the aspects of India that I enjoyed so much. The Indian people seemed so glad to have me there.

Although I do not regret buying bottled water whenever I did not have purification tablets handy for my canteen, I must have an iron stomach because I never suffered ill effects from water in all of my travels.

৯৵৽

Another memorable bargaining session I had, in reverse, was in Libya. My shoes had worn out and I needed another pair. I looked in shops that sold shoes, but those for women were cloth things entirely unsuitable for my feet for the tough desert conditions where I intended to walk. In a shop featuring men's sandals I found just what I wanted—good leather soles—or maybe the sole was cut out of tire but tough—and straps nailed firmly to the soles. I expected these would succor my feet.

From Istanbul on, these shoe shops are for both making the goods and selling them, sort of holes-in-the-wall with open fronts that have rollup metal doors, open by day for business and closed by night. Sometimes I saw women vending on the streets, but in these shops, men seemed to be the ones who made sandals, tin ware, leather goods, or sewed clothes. They worked at their craft until a customer came in, then tended to the bargaining as needed.

I pointed to a pair that looked about my size, supposing he would give me the first price and we'd go on from there. Instead he shook his head. Then I put money in my palm but he still shook his head. I added some. No. By grunts and signs, I understood why he was not trying to sell me the shoes, even refusing when I tried to buy: These were for men. He thought I was making a mistake, that I was unaware of their intended purpose.

An honest merchant! Actually, in all my travels, if I ever met any dishonest merchants who cheated me, I never recognized it.

I tried to indicate that I knew they were for men but wanted them nonetheless. This went on for quite a while. But I *needed* those shoes, so persisted, the reverse of bargaining being that I kept adding more money in my hand for them. He was almost as persistent but finally capitulated, I think not from greed at the high price he was getting as much as just thinking I was too stubborn to quit.

The shoes fit perfectly and I was quite happy with them, but I knew he was sad despite the good price—that was still far less than sandals of equivalent quality would have cost in the United States—because he felt that he had cheated me.

It was not until some time later that I learned that in the Muslim world it is sinful for men and women to cross dress and he was trying his best to prevent me from that sin. I was glad I did not know this at the time for, I might have been tempted to forego my own needs to respect his beliefs. But I really needed those shoes!

৯৵৽

I seldom ate in restaurants, though of course I had no alternative sometimes. Instead, I bought food that did not need to be cooked or that was already cooked from food vendors.

In Great Britain, I did not find food, other than tea, noteworthy. In France I had an amazing discovery—bread—good, crusty bread that really was my staff of life and cheap, too.

After that, what I found called French bread or Italian bread in the States had little relation to "the real thing." That discovery of bread has remained one of the most important results of all my travels. After coming home with the happy memory of that bread, I sadly discovered that finding the same sort, un-sliced, unwrapped European style, is just not possible in many places here.

Traveling spoiled me about bread, for I knew after that that our common soft, sliced, plastic-wrapped bread here is just—ersatz!

With bread, I usually had cheese, *good* cheese, not the ersatz processed kind in plastic wrap. People so often asked how I could afford so much travel abroad. When I answered, "Bread!" "Cheese!" "Pasta!" or "Rice!" they were puzzled. Their image of those foodstuffs as produced here in the States simply could not serve as basic and filling and satisfying food.

In Belgium and the Netherlands I discovered another accompaniment for bread for breakfast: chocolate sandwiches. A plain Hershey bar between two slices of (good!) bread is such a good breakfast!

In Denmark I adored those exquisite Danish pastries, better and lighter than here. In every Danish town, I made a zigzag course down its streets, getting a small, light pastry at every shop. That never spoiled my appetite for more solid bread and cheese at mealtime!

In Germany, you could still find crusty wheat bread, but there good solid pumpernickel was popular, though I did not find it superior to American pumpernickel loaves, except I enjoyed that the Germans did not slice it. Maybe it is the atavistic savage in me that feels more satisfied to eat bread in hunks.

Good German salami-like preserved meats made a delicious accompaniment to the bread.

Italy's great offering was her pasta and the wonderful tomato-and-spinach pies (pizza). I was fond of a spinach pie there that I found more solid and satisfying than quiche. My favorite food in Italy was the large cup of cappuccino coffee for breakfast served with a roll with butter and jelly. I do not know if the tradition persists today, but back then, stores would sell a blob of butter and another of jelly wrapped in a torn piece of newspaper to eat with the roll.

Breakfast in Greece was a bowl of warm milk and honey served with good bread. All very common foods for here, too, but the difference, I think, was in the bread.

Another food encounter delighted me in Amsterdam, the Netherlands. I was walking down the street, looking avidly at whatever there was to see, when suddenly I wheeled about. Something had caught my eye in a store window with neat labels—*pinda kaas*. My mind translated—peanut cheese—peanut butter! Of course, I bought a jar, not having realized until that moment that it was the first—and turned out, last—peanut butter I found outside the United States. Not that I ever looked for it; after all I was there to see or taste the "custom of the country." It made me pause, though.

New world corn and yams have taken over Africa as staples, and potatoes are ubiquitous in all Europe, except Italy. Why have peanuts and peanut butter not become common in these countries in the same way?

Mention of potatoes reminds me of the chips of England, similar to what we call French fries. The now-common fish-and-chips frozen plates of the United States are inferior. I had never heard of eggs and chips, but that being cheaper than fish and chips, I had that dish more often in the United Kingdom. They also had several kinds of fish available; the name did not signify only one kind. Another common dish in Britain was sausage and mashed potatoes instead of fish and chips.

In Germany I never saw potatoes prepared as chips. *Kartoffeln* ("potatoes") were all over Germany but not as mashed there either, as I recall. There potatoes were boiled and eaten with salt and butter, but never pepper, or else with sort of oil and other ingredients with, which I guess was "German potato salad." Regardless of how Germans prepared potatoes, though, I never heard different names for different ways that they were prepared—only *Kartoffeln*.

The German potato salad (*Kartoffelsalat*) is not especially like what comes to mind when we hear the term in the United States. How potato salad is prepared in Germany varies widely by region.

Fortunately, I like just about any food and can make a satisfying meal from whatever is available. Like that peanut butter that I had not missed until I noticed it in Amsterdam, or the milk in Seattle after having dried in Alaska, I never found myself missing familiar foods while I was on the road.

I did miss familiar meal *times* though, being quite accustomed to having my dinner around five thirty in the evening every day. By contrast, in Europe and Latin America (where I had to be more dependent on restaurants), dinner is typically served closer to eight o'clock in the evening. I starved during the two hours between when my stomach wanted a meal and when it was available. Then I would dream of home, where I could eat at my leisure.

When I finally arrived home though, what did I find?

My appetite had acclimated to lateness. I began taking dinner around seven thirty. The perversity of human nature—appetite!

In another part of the globe, I found I did not even need meal-time acclimation, even though the custom was also very different from my normal three a day. In the Buddhist *vihara* where I stayed awhile in India and then in Myanmar, they eat a two a day: morning rice and afternoon rice, about nine in the morning and then again around four in the afternoon.

I cannot begin to know the way the Buddhists fixed the rice but I knew that it satisfied my hunger. I was never hungry as long as I was there. Those meals were vegetarian, and I never missed meat then either.

In Pakistan the basic meal is rice seasoned with curry. The first two or three meals I found the hot chili-pepper curry *too* spicy hot. But hunger makes me willing to eat anything, and before long my stomach had acclimated and I grew to love rice seasoned with curry.

The curry was of two kinds: dal or meat. Dal curry is a thick, creamy East Indian stew made with lentils or other legumes, and onions. I would never have thought to spice lentils with curry, but over rice, it was quite tasty.

Meat curry can be prepared with a variety of meats—any but beef I guess—but what I had must have been mostly goat meat in a sort of curry stew over the rice—an even better a meal!

With dal or meat curry, Indians usually ate a bread called *chapatti*. *Chapatti* is prepared from plain wheat flour, but not like any wheat flour I ever saw here. The flour is moistened with water just enough to allow kneading. Then the dough is patted into flapjack-looking small portions and cooked in a large skillet-like (but flatter) pan directly over a flame until done on one side, then flipped and cooked on the other side. I never saw one burned. I did not much care for *chapatti*, and with rice it seemed unnecessary, so I did not eat *chapatti* much.

There were two other kinds of *chapatti* that I did love in India. *Poori* is a *chapatti* fried in oil, and *roti*, which I never did quite figure out how it was different from ordinary *chapatti*, but ate with relish even so.

The best food of India was the yogurt-based *lhassi*. It was sweet and I drank lots because I believed it to be healthful, but more because I enjoyed it so much. Granted, I knew *lhassi* was made from yogurt, and that yogurt is made from a kind of fermentation of milk, but when I returned to the United States someone told me that *lhassi* had an alcoholic content. At first I thought perhaps that I had experienced my first alcoholic "glow." No wonder I liked India best of all the foreign countries I had visited! Even after learning that *lhassi* is not alcoholic, I continued to smile at the playful ruse, and *lhassi* remains one of my all-time favorite beverages.

My most memorable food encounter happened in Addis Ababa, Ethiopia. I was there with a group of United States professors studying education in Africa. The Ethiopian Ministry of Education treated us to a dinner at the finest restaurant in Addis Ababa, at tables of four, three Americans and some bureaucrat of the ministry for the international exchange.

If I had thought Indian curry spicy hot, I had not yet tasted Ethiopian food. That was *really* hot, from what I never found out. I never did learn to like those spices as I had learned to like curry.

The meal was served with a drink called *tej*, the Ehtiopian version of mead, made by fermenting honey, water, and yeast with flavorings such as herbs, spices, or flowers. Mead dates back to biblical time; it was known to the classical Romans and Greeks.

At that meal, as it was alcoholic, I never drank the *tej*. I usually carried a canteen of water supposedly purified by tablets, but it seemed gauche to bring out my canteen at the formal dinner. I supposed that I could opt for a soft drink, or their purified water—no luck! So I suffered a bit until I could get back to some water, but that was not the strange encounter at all.

The plate was the common Ethiopian bits of meat in gravy—like stew. I supposed that I would rather not know if the meat was from goat or camel or whatever. Although the taste was not appealing to me, I ate half-zestfully anyway, but noticed that the other two Americans at my table ate only a small bit. When we all but finished, the bureaucrat casually mentioned that the meat was cat.

One of my group fled to the rest room and the other turned green. I kept eating to finish the plate. My companion whispered in tones of horror, "I guess you did not hear him say it's (gasp!) *cat meat!*"

I said yes, I had heard, and to his wonder, took the last bite or two to finish the plate. He was clearly aghast but too polite to continue his comments. I was surprised, yes, and if I could have read the menu, I might not have ordered cat meat, but *that* it was cat meat made no particular difference to me than the meat of any other animal, cow, pig, or chicken. I never did see much of a difference.

Two or three years later on a Sioux reservation, I was with some Sioux who, knowing Anglo food prejudices against eating dog, told me beforehand that was being served so that I could decline if I wished. I do not recall whether there was an alternate meat offered, but I ate the dog and the Sioux did not mention it again. I have wondered ever since whether the Sioux thought I was silly trying to show off or if they admired that some Caucasians would share their food.

Ordinarily I will eat anything that sane people normally eat.

෧෧

I have forgotten what town it was in Peru that I had what I call "the income tax encounter." I was visiting a school. My guide, the principal, apologized for its poorness—saying the United States had refused to send more money down to improve it. I did *not* scream in some sort of rage at the constant blame of the United States for every ill. I just pointed out that the women teachers there were wearing clothes that were obviously more expensive than what I was wearing.

Why was I so poor I could not afford as fine clothes as theirs? Because I had paid such a high percentage of my salary in income tax. Yes, salaries in the United States are high compared to Peru, but when the income tax is deducted, they become more comparable.

A factor that accounted for higher salaries in the United States compared with some other countries, as I saw it, was that American teachers do very much more than teachers abroad do. This may not be so true in Europe, but I saw in the Soviet Union and in third world schools that teachers caused tardy starts more often than students did, and early dismissals and long frequent recesses were expected.

The income tax concept astounded the principal. He had never heard of the concept. He asked me if I would mind telling the staff about it. I agreed, and school was dismissed early so that the teachers could hear me. In the United States, more likely teachers would be required to stay after students were dismissed at the usual time. The teachers marveled at the notion of income tax. I marveled at their ignorance of where the United States Government got the money it sent to countries such as theirs for aid. How did they finance their own governments?

That got me wondering how United States financed government before the income tax was established in 1913. Taxes on imports? Sales tax? Property taxes? Taxes certainly have been with us for millennia but just not on income apparently.

Just another of the abysmal depths of my ignorance! To think I was surprised at theirs! How shallow of me.

It was not the teachers' ignorance of our income tax system that bothered me as much as their calm assumption that the United States or some entity other than they *ought* to pay for their needs. While I believe that a need for one of us is a need for all of us on one level, we all have a duty to be self-responsible too, each individual and each nation.

I suppose I still cannot, even after all my time abroad, really quite accept that I am a very privileged individual. I was never hungry as a child, I had access to a good education, my family instilled a solid work ethic in me so that when I took a job I could hold it. Above all, to have been born into a nation with a healthy economy that provides jobs was a great privilege.

ஓௗௗ

There were many other encounters for such a bagful of mixed memories here half a century or so later. At Stratford-upon-Avon, I was about to put my shilling in the turnstile to enter Charlecote Manor and Park where William Shakespeare was said to have poached deer when suddenly—though I am the soul of honesty and integrity—I thought of asserting my kinship with the Bard by poaching entrance. So I went a bit along the wall and climbed over. If caught I would confess and throw myself on the mercy of the British sense of humor. I was not caught.

I recall no other particular thrill about the rest of my touristy visit to Avon, except the performance that night of *The Merchant of Venice*. That was my first world-class performance of a Shakespeare play. I was hooked immediately.

Besides Shakespeare in England, I tried to catch the national greatness of the various countries in their performing arts. This was sometimes frustrating, as, for example, in Dublin, Ireland, I went to see the Book of Kells, an Irish manuscript containing the Four Gospels, a fragment of Hebrew names, and the Eusebian canons.

Where was the great book when I arrived? On tour in the United States. Not that tour but one again a decade or two later I did see it in New York.

Then I went to see the Royal Danish Ballet. The ballet was not there either. So where? On tour in the United States. Not that tour but one a decade or so later I saw it in New York.

I got a consolation prize in Århus, Denmark. While their national performing art treasure was on tour in the United States, an American opera treasure, George Gershwin's *Porgy and Bess*, was on tour there. I think likely I would not have gone to see the play here—after all, I had not gone in its already some years since it hit the boards—but I did there.

Even though I missed the Royal Danish Ballet while I was in Denmark, later I did see the Moscow Ballet as well as some opera there. I think that Russian opera is "borrowed" from the European tradition, so I do not count that as a "treasure of the country."

When I was in Calcutta I met that great treasure of Bengal and of all the world, Nobel Laureate Rabindranath Tagore. I had never heard of him or his work before my trip. Tagore wrote thousands of poems and dozens of plays. I caught the *King of the Dark Chamber*, with his trademark blazing crimson flames purifying the soul and purifying the society—I have never seen a stage production so *powerful* since. I caught another Tagore performance years later in New York.

࿓

A moment of noble solemn resolve remains strong in my memory. It was in the Paris hostel the first week of May 1956—just ten years after World War II and the devastating holocaust—very soon after I first began my travels. I was the only American present, but I recall that there were two or three folks from Australia, New Zealand, Great Britain, just about every country in Western Europe; possibly an Eastern European, but no Soviets; some from South Africa; an Israeli, a North African Arab—a general world mix. This wide range of homelands represented is common to most hostels most of the time, but that night in Paris seemed to gather more of a mix than usual, especially having Germans among Dutch, French, and neutral Swedes.

Talk turned to just ten years before, when we had been fighting each other to the death. The Germans among us almost cried thinking of the terrible evil Nazi Germany had spread.

That day the solemn resolve among us was that even as we had been caught in war, in evil, once that had made us enemies, so now in the spirit of genuine friendship we forged that moment would we do all in our power to ensure that our countries would never again war with each other—or with any other nations—from now into the future. For that hour in a Paris hostel, we shared the age-old dream of peace and goodwill.

I had thought about peace before—who has not?—but have thought about it more ever since that night in Paris.

STUDY QUESTIONS

1. The solemn experience that the author shared with an international group she found in the Paris hostel happened in 1956, very shortly after she first began her travel.

- Why do you think that the author waiting until the end of her book to relate this experience?
- Would you characterize the author's experience in Paris as spiritual, religious, or some other way?
- Define and differentiate spiritual experience and religious experience, and discuss whether you believe the author values either or both. Cite examples from the text to support your position.

2. The author makes statements in different places that indicate her values with regard to sexuality.

- Citing specific examples from the text, discuss what values are suggested both by the encounters described and the language chosen to form the descriptions.
- Do the author's actions during her travel and her action in the form of writing the memoirs appear to be consistent with her stated sense of modesty and morality? Cite specific examples.
- Discuss the relevance of Gertrude's statement in *Hamlet*, "the lady doth protest too much, methinks," to the author's self-perception regarding sexuality. Use specific citations from the text to support your position.

3. Instructing South American teachers about American income tax, the author states that she marveled at their ignorance of where the United States Government got the money it sent to countries such as theirs for aid.

- Compare and contrast the author's implicit attitude toward needy nations and toward the United States when she began her travels with the one implicit in the above passage.

Nine

EPILOGUE

My travels have taken me over a large portion of our tiny global home and I am wildly in love with it and with the peoples who live on it, with all their faults and horrors. I went abroad looking for answers and came home with even more questions.

I still ponder whether my principles of human decency should include pacifism, or whether the world being what it is with so many peoples who have not yet ascended enough to respect common decency, instead inflicting evils on the world such as the Holocaust and other acts of genocide, that war in some cases remains the lesser of two monstrous evils. About some vital issues we may need to remain resigned to uncertainty.

In the Soviet Union the Intourist guides (guards?) were always harping on: *mir e druzbah* ("peace and friendship"). I knew that "peace" for the Soviets meant the time when the world would have become Communist with Moscow as the world capital—ignoring that there was in its history hardly any "peace" among the various Communist factions and parties.

I reflected on *pax Romana*, meaning bowing to Rome and its edicts without revolt; during that time Rome still fought a number of wars against neighboring states and tribes.

Then *pax Britannica*, meaning when the sun never set on the British Empire and the subject peoples accepted without open revolt.

To my way of thinking, that such "peace" is no peace at all for the subject peoples is obvious; instead they are merely bowing in mute resignation to power. With any peace worth the name, there has to be also—*justice*.

❧

Finally, after many months, I landed in Newport News, Virginia, back in the U.S.A. *Pax Americana?*—not period but question mark. I had concluded that I had found just the opposite of what I went abroad to find. I concluded that idealism is unrealistic. I had gone looking for ways better than the United States had done because despite all its lofty wording, I believed that we had secured the pursuit of happiness and justice for only some. I had found—such a society does not exist, except as an abstract concept that lives in our minds, for which we can strive if we have the will, and strive for better if we garner a collective will marked by shared wholesome values.

Some people may believe that the United States has miserable, grievous failings, but I did not find better elsewhere. Some may contend that Norway and

Sweden have "got it" better than we do, but there people are homogenous in ethnicity and religion. They do not face the challenges that we face, so the situations are not analogous. In addition, I saw high rates of alcoholism and suicide in those countries. Sometimes I heard the argument that suicide is a human right not yet recognized by some societies. I suppose I did not want to be convinced.

I believe that the United States offers what I see as the most chance for that elusive pursuit of abundance and happiness to more of its people than I observed in any other society. I can only hope that our notion of *pax Americana* will be marked by justice and not abuse of power. I hope that corporate CEOs will not typically view corporate interests as national interests. I hope that our minorities will not be disenfranchised.

So many problems!

I do not know how to begin to solve the problems facing our complex society, or even to live happily knowing that we have no solutions.

But then, happiness is not what we are guaranteed by the Constitution, only the pursuit of happiness. That is the American dream, is it not?

I confess that I still simply do not know what the "American" dream is. Is the "American dream" any different in essentials from some African tribal group's dream? But this question begs another: What is "essential"?

Did Martin Luther King dream of the demise of segregation and racism only in this country, making that an American dream for him? These are subjective issues. Others might dream differently, still believing that their dream is, like our dream, for the country's good. Was King's dream for the Americans or for whole human race?

Thinking about that "American way of life," how much can our way of life change and still be the "American way"? Just in my lifetime, my "way of life" has changed beyond any recognition, as surely it has for the vast majority of Americans. Technology has vastly changed daily life for most people in the world. Such change is bound to continue, so how can we talk of *the* "American way" when that way is constantly changing? I am not satisfied to hear some earnest explanation that some change due to technological innovation, such as laptop computers, is just a surface change, but that the real core of American values that we hold with pride has not changed.

"American values"? Values do change. I have seen our values change drastically during my lifetime. For example, the notion that racism is evil is relatively new, significantly changed in this country over the course of my lifetime. In the first half of the twentieth century, I am sure most whites in the segregated South never considered themselves as evil, sinful racists. They viewed segregation as the right way to live. Neither did most Northerners, who pointed fingers south in holier-than-thou opposition dream that they, too, might be considered racist, even where de jure segregation was not practiced. Yet now the American ideal holds that racism in any form is evil.

The crux of the matter is that I believe that in order for us to progress as a civilization, Americans and citizens of all countries ought to begin to think of "our good" as the good of all humanity and not restrict our thought only to what is good for our own country.

About this I am certain. If we are to survive in this age of such frightening technology, we must strive to ascend toward a life as symbolized by baptism into a more principled, abundant life—and keep on ascending—so that humankind shall not perish from this beautiful bountiful small globe spinning in space—space travel or colonization notwithstanding—the only home humankind shall ever have, I think. This is my human, beyond American, dream.

I am so grateful that I chose this country as my home.

To say "chose" was no mistake, though I am a citizen by birth. I came to know at Newport News, as I finished my "real" travel abroad (as opposed to commercial group touring), aware that I was making a conscious choice now to live in this country, not a citizen only by accident of birth, but by act of free will.

It has been said that the best part of traveling is to be back home again and so true—I am back home in the United States of America, my home, my heart, my very self.

STUDY QUESTIONS

1. The author states that she went traveling because she was dissatisfied with the faults she found in America but ends her memoirs with the claim, "I am wildly in love with [Earth] and with the peoples who live on it, with all their faults and horrors."

   - Do these two statements embody inconsistent concurrent values, a change of opinion, or some other state of affairs?
   - If you believe that the author changed her mind, what experiences transpired that caused the author to change her opinion?

2. The author states, "To my way of thinking, that such 'peace' is no peace at all for the subject peoples is obvious; instead they are merely bowing in mute resignation to power. With any peace worth the name there has to be also—*justice*."

   - What values underlie this statement?
   - Does the author imply that colonialism is unjust?

3. The author states, "I do not know how to begin to solve the problems facing our complex society, or even to live happily knowing that we have no solutions."

   - Does this statement imply that the author has not achieved happiness?

4. The author states, "If we are to survive in this age of such frightening technology, we must strive to ascend toward a life as symbolized by baptism, into a more principled abundant life."
- What does the author mean by "life as symbolized by baptism"?
- In real terms, what actions would exemplify striving as envisioned by the author?

5. The author asks, "Thinking about that "American way of life," how much can our way of life change and still be the "American way?"
- Discuss your answer to the author's question.

6. The author provides evidence of her values and attitudes by statements she makes about her experiences, by her choice of places to travel and sites to see, and by her actions described while on her journey. Writing per se is also an action and as such embodies values held by the author.
- Citing specific examples from the text, demonstrate a value that is consistently portrayed across all four modes of expression and a case where inconsistency is evident from one mode to another.
- Discuss evidence in the text that supports or refutes the hypothesis that the author was naive or unsophisticated. Cite textual examples to support your position.
- What evidence can you cite that speaks to the author's sense of humor? Can you point to passages that appear to indicate naiveté but might instead be open to interpretation as intentional appearance of callowness with a "wink"?
- Extra credit: Write a list of values held by the author, stated or implied, and indicate whether you believe this author cherished, abhorred, or was neutral toward them as traits for her or others. For each value, cite specific examples, stating whether the author's actions were consistent with her self-perception and/or her self-assessment.

7. After returning from her travels, the author said, "I chose this country as my home . . . not a citizen only by accident of birth, but by act of free will."
- Do you believe that the author felt more satisfied with America after returning from her travels than before she left?
- How do you think her view of the United States changed over time?
- Did the author's values, judgments, or perception of reality change over time?
- Cite specific experiences that the author describes that contributed the changes she made in her thinking and judgments.

FOR FURTHER READING

Barlett, Donald L., and James B. Steele. *America: What Went Wrong?* Kansas City, Mo.: Andrews and McMeel, 1992.
   Details how Wall Street dealmakers changed the rules to favor the privileged.

Brown, Dee Alexander. *Bury My Heart at Wounded Knee: An Indian History of the American West.* New York: Holt, 1991.
   Recounts how the American Indians lost their land, culture, and lives.

Brown, Les. *Live Your Dreams.* New York: Morrow, 1992.
   Proposes that anyone can succeed by stoking the fires of hunger for a dream.

Brzezinski, Zbigniew. *The Grand Failure: The Birth and Death of Communism in the Twentieth Century.* New York: Scribner, 1989.
   Summarizes the history of Soviet Communism.

Fletcher, Joseph F. *Situation Ethics: The New Morality.* Philadelphia, Pa.: Westminster Press, 1966.
   Holds that some acts may be morally right, depending on the circumstances.

Franck, Harry Alverson. *A Vagabond Journey around the World: A Narrative of Personal Experience.* New York: Appleton-Century, 1910.
   Worked his way around the world mingling with common people.

Goodwin, Jan. *Price of Honor: Muslim Women Lift the Veil of Silence on the Islamic World.* Boston, Mass.: Little, Brown, 1994.
   Surveys ten countries in the Islamic world, concluding that the treatment of women is a barometer of the twin forces of modernity and Islamic extremism.

Halliburton, Richard. *New Worlds to Conquer.* Indianapolis, Ind.: Bobbs-Merrill, 1929.
   Details Halliburton's exploration of South America.

Harris, Dixie Lee. "Certain Aspects of Native Education in the Americas in the 1960s." PhD diss., Syracuse University, 1970.
   Observations made during on-site visits to schools in North/South America.

Hawkins, Gerald S. *Stonehenge Decoded.* Garden City, N.Y.: Doubleday, 1965.
   Solves the mystery of purpose of Stonehenge, to predict celestial events.

Hooks, Bell. *Killing Rage: Ending Racism.* New York: Holt, 1995.
   Offers a black and feminist perspective on the issue of race in America.

Jamison, Kay R. *Exuberance: The Passion for Life.* New York: Knopf, 2004.
   Examines the contagious nature of exuberance: "Those who are exuberant act."

Kasser, Tim. *The High Price of Materialism*. Cambridge, Mass.: MIT Press, 2002.
    Describes the scientific evidence relating to materialism and happiness.

Lappé, Frances Moore. *Rediscovering America's Values*. New York: Ballantine, 1989.
    Encourages Americans to find solutions for themselves.

McKeon, Richard Peter. "Symposia," *Proceedings and Addresses of the American Philosophical Association*, 25 (September 1952): 42–60.
    Discusses the role of table talk in the history of philosophy.

Moran, Edward, ed. *The Global Ecology*. New York: H. W. Wilson, 1999.
    Frames the issues of ecology, offering some technical considerations, personal testimonies, and possible solutions to the ecology crisis.

Nanji, Azim. *The Muslim Almanac: A Reference Work on the History, Faith, Culture, and Peoples of Islam*. Detroit, Mich.: Gale Research, 1996.
    Additional discussion of the customs and culture of the Muslim world.

Nash, Roderick. *The Rights of Nature: A History of Environmental Ethics*. Madison: University of Wisconsin Press, 1989.
    Traces the origin of environmental ethics.

Polo, Marco. *The Adventures of Marco Polo*. Edited by Richard J. Walsh, illustrated by Cyrus Le Roy. New York: John Day Co., 1948.
    Tells of journeys along the Silk Road to China.

Saint-Exupéry, Antoine de. *Night Flight*. New York: Harcourt Brace Jovanovich, 1974.
    Tale about flying the mail to remote areas of the Andes Mountains.

Tagore, Rabindranath. *Collected Poems and Plays of Rabindranath Tagore*. New York: Macmillan, 1937.
    Works of the Nobel Laureate Rabindranath Tagore.

Terkel, Studs. *The Great Divide: Second Thoughts on the American Dream*. New York: Pantheon Books, 1988.
    Discussion of the divide between haves and have-nots in America.

Thomas, Lowell Jackson, Jr. *Out of This World: Across the Himalayas to Forbidden Tibet*. New York: Greystone, 1950.
    Diary of travel to Tibet and documentation of Tibetan life before the Chinese invasion.

UNESCO. *World Heritage: Monumental Sites*. Paris: UNESCO, 2004.
    Guide to sites designated by the UNESCO World Heritage project.

Wilder, Thornton, *The Bridge of San Luis Rey*. New York: Grosset & Dunlap, 1927.
    After a bridge collapses, the author asks, "Why did this happen to those five?"

ABOUT THE AUTHOR

Dixie Lee Harris was born in Arkansas and spent her early years on a cotton farm during the Great Depression in the United States. She attended public schools, then took the BS in chemistry from Arkansas State College (now Arkansas State University), Jonesboro, Arkansas, in 1946. Her first job was as an industrial chemist in Oak Ridge, Tennessee. She then took a job as a chemist in Beacon, New York.

Dissatisfied with a career as a chemist, Harris took the MA in education from Columbia University Teacher's College, New York, New York, in 1955. Between 1955 and 1967, she traveled the world, visiting approximately sixty-seven different countries. During 1957–1960, she taught school in Alaska, during which time she was able to combine her avocation to teach with her urge to experience geographic "ultimates," such as hiking at the Arctic Circle and the northernmost point of the United States.

In 1970, Harris took the PhD from Syracuse University, Syracuse, New York, upon presentation of a dissertation titled "Certain Aspects of Native Education in the Americas in the 1960s." After completing her doctoral work, she worked as a teacher in the New York State prison system at the Beacon Correctional Facility in Beacon, New York.

During the last ten years of her working career, Harris was elected as a union representative and then elected to the Executive Board of the Public Employees Federation of New York State.

Harris is the author of *Twenty Stories of Bible Women* (Hauppauge, N.Y.: Exposition Press, 1980). Throughout her life, she has been interested in civil liberties, peace, labor issues, and feminism. She has been an avid enthusiast of camping, hiking, and writing. She continued to attend college courses of interest and to take brief study trips around the world until 2005.

She characterizes her life as lived "during war, prosperity, exuberant living, and occasional crises."

INDEX

Abraham (Ibrihim), 112
adventure(s), 1, 4, 11, 28, 35, 36, 45, 88
aesthetics, 90, 100, 102, 104, 117
affluence, 88
Afghanistan, 19, 20, 23, 47, 48, 80, 95
Africa, 63, 68, 95, 118, 121, 122
Afro-Americans, 64
Ajanta caves, 104–106
Alaska, 11–13, 26, 31–43, 50, 58, 121
Alaska Marine Highway, 33
Alaskan Railroad, 35
Alcan Highway, 11, 13, 52
Algeria, 68–74
Alhambra, 68
Allah (the Compassionate), 83–85, 98,
    112, 113
Allenby Bridge, 13
alms giving, 60
Alps, Swiss, 99
Altiplano, 56, 89
Amazon River, 48, 50, 61–63
Andeans, ancient, 90
Andes Mountains, 56, 57, 61, 89, 90,
    94, 108
Angkor Wat, 111
Annunciation, 16
Antarctica, 2
Appalachian Trail, 107
appreciation (appreciated), 56, 95, 96,
    98, 101, 104
aqueduct(s), 100
Arab countries, 14
architecture, 76, 98, 100, 103, 104, 113,
    114
Arctic Circle, 32, 35, 43, 133
Arctic Ocean, 35
Argentina, 57, 87
Aristotle, 42, 79
Arizona, 25, 114
art, 91, 98, 103, 104, 117, 118, 125
Asia, 46, 55, 58, 89, 118
Atatürk, Mustafa Kemal, 8, 76

Athapascans, 26, 36
Athena, 102
Athos, Mount, 7
Australia, 2, 23, 125
autonomy, 15, 23

Babylon, 112
Babylonian captivity, 55
Bachelor Officers Quarters (BOQ), 31,
    34
backpacking, 6
Bangladesh, 57
bank(ing)(s), 40, 59, 69, 72
Baranof Island, 31
bargaining, 118, 119
Bay of Bengal, 57, 59, 83
Beaufort Sea, 43
beauty, 46, 58, 91–93, 95, 100, 103–
    106, 110
begging bowl, 110
belief(s), 29, 55, 59, 60, 80, 84, 86, 101,
    106, 107, 110, 119
bells, 23, 58, 110
biblical site, 114
blessedness, 85
blossoms, 57, 92
boat(s), 22, 23, 44, 50, 51, 58–60, 62,
    63, 109, 111
Bolivia, 48, 56, 90
Book of Kells, 125
border(s), 4. *See also* frontier(s)
    Afghan, 19, 23, 48
    Columbian, 24
    Malaysian, 23
    Sudan, 60
    Syrian, 23
    U.S./Canadian, 44, 56
    Yukon, 11, 12
Bosra, Cathedral of, 113
braids, coronet, 25, 27
Brazil, 50–52, 61, 62, 87
bridge(s), 13, 44, 45, 50, 51, 65, 92

bristlecone pines, 93
British Columbia, 43
British Empire, 127
Brits, 18, 71
Brooklyn Museum of Art, 117
Bryant, William Cullen, 55
Buddha, 58, 110–112
Buddhi(sm)(sts), 55, 58, 59, 80, 82, 84,
       104, 105, 109–111, 121
Bureau of Indian Affairs (BIA), 33, 36, 37
Burma. *See* Myanmar
burning ghat, 80. *See* Manikarnika Ghat
burqa(s), 72, 74, 76–78, 80, 85, 86
Buryat Republic, 55

Cahokia Mounds, 108
caldera(s), 95
California, 26, 52, 91, 93
camaraderie, 53
Cambodia, 111
camping, 11, 14, 45
Canada, 11, 12, 39, 43
Canon del Pato, 90
Canyon de Chelly, 114, 115
capitalism, 54, 66
cargo, 64, 95
    human, 60
Caribbean Ocean, 94
carving(s), 104–106, 111, 112
Casbah, 68
Cathay, 46
Catskill/Delaware Mountain watershed,
       100
cave(s), 104, 105
chador(s), 72, 74
chaitaya(s), 104
Chalkidiki Peninsula, 8
Charlecote Manor and Park, 124
checkpoint, frontier, 6, 24
Chelsea Pumping Station, 100, 104, 116
Chile, 43, 44, 46, 56, 57, 90
chimes, 58
China, 2, 46, 58
    Indochina, 57
Christianity, 112

Orthodox, 55
church(es), 38, 55, 75, 76, 100, 111, 113
Church, Frederick Edwin, 90
Circle Hot Springs, 43
citizen(s)(ship), 1, 12, 17, 19, 25, 28,
       38, 65, 71, 73, 129, 130
civilization(s), 14, 47, 103, 111, 129
class(ism), 24, 62, 65
cliff dwellings, Pueblo, 114
climate, 18, 58
climbing, 91, 109, 112
Coast Guard, U.S., 13, 32, 39
coca, 56
cold, 18, 34, 48, 49, 56, 57, 94
colon(ies)(y), 31, 129
Colorado, 93
Columbia, 24, 39, 43, 89, 108, 109
comfort, 5, 7, 10, 23, 50, 51, 53, 56, 60,
       62, 64, 75, 88, 92
common sense, 36
communication, 2, 79, 81, 108
Communis(m)(ts), 5, 6, 10, 17–19, 25,
       41, 54, 55, 80, 127
communit(ies)(y), 32, 67, 75, 114
confluence(s), 61
conifers, 91
conscience, 6, 23, 118
consent, informed, 80
consequence(s), 28, 71, 97, 102, 116
Constantine the Great, 13
consul(ate), 10, 16, 17, 23
conversation(s), 5, 54, 63, 72, 77, 79
cooperation, 105
Cordilleras, Occidental/Oriental, 89
corruption, 61
cosmos, 118
cost(s), 5, 6, 34, 49, 54, 61, 64, 66, 97,
       98, 115, 119
"Cotopaxi!" (Church), 90
Council of the Gods, 102
Covenant, Ark of, 112
Crater Lake, 95
Creation of Humankind, 102
Creator, 95
crew(s) member(s), 35, 70, 97

cruzeiros, 61
culture, 17, 26, 40, 48, 59, 75, 77, 79,
    82, 92, 103, 111, 115
curiosity, 1, 18, 43, 65, 94, 106
currency, 3, 4, 6, 7, 69, 70
custom(s), 37, 38, 40, 59, 75, 77, 78,
    80, 82, 111, 119, 121
customs, 8, 9, 57

Dalai Lamas, Tibetan, 48
Dalton Highway, 43
danger, 21, 31, 32, 51, 73
Danube River, 4, 6, 28
Darien Gap, 43
Dead Sea, 47
Decapolis, 15
decency, 107, 114, 127
deck(s), 58–61, 64
deit(ies)(y), 84, 96, 107, 110, 111, 117
demon(s), 111
Denmark, 120, 125
dinars, 4, 5, 7
disaster(s), 79
disillusionment, 54, 63
desire, 11, 15, 19, 59, 62, 80, 84, 97
Divinity, 90, 94, 95–99, 110, 118
Dome of the Rock, 112, 113
Dominican Republic, 3, 4
Druid(ism)(s), 106, 107
Duomo of Milan, 99, 101, 102

economic system, 66, 80
Eddy, Nelson, 12
Edgecumbe, Mount, 31
education, 3, 17, 37, 38, 81, 122, 124
effort, 58, 71, 94, 97–99, 111, 114
Egypt(ians), 16, 60, 68, 101, 102, 106, 109
eight-fold path, 110
Eisenhower, Dwight D., 53
Elgin marbles, 103
Elgin, Lord, 103
Elisha's Fountain, 14
Ellora caves, 104–106
embass(ies)(y), 4, 6, 20, 21, 48, 104
employees, federal, 41

encounter(s), 3, 4, 7, 8, 10–14, 17, 19, 21,
    23–30, 64, 67, 68, 71, 73, 117,
    118, 120, 122, 123, 124, 126
energy, 102, 106, 117
England, 106, 111, 121, 124
enmity, 9, 114
Eritrea, 49
Eskimos, 40
essence, 98, 102
eternity, 97
ethics, 6, 28, 37, 116
Ethiopia, 49, 68, 122, 123
Ethiopian Ministry of Education, 122
ethnography, 117, 118
Europe(ans), 1, 1, 11, 21, 23, 16, 55, 63,
    64, 118, 120, 121, 123, 125
Eusebian canons, 125
evil(s), 65, 79, 97, 125, 127, 128
expenses, 15, 40
experience(s), 2–4, 7, 8, 22, 27, 28, 35–
    37, 41, 45–47, 51, 54, 58, 59,
    63, 64, 66–68, 71, 74, 77, 87,
    88, 90–92, 94, 95, 99, 102, 107,
    109, 115, 117, 126, 129, 130

faith(s), 49, 104
fear, 4, 6, 16, 73, 85, 87, 97, 116
Federal Aviation Administration
    (FAA), 32
Federico Costa, 63, 64
festival(s), 108
Fifth International Conference of
    American States, 44
fjord(s), 11
flight(s), 32, 35, 40, 41
Florida, 3, 17, 25, 57
fluency, 24, 72
fluvial network, 22, 23, 58, 59
foreigner(s), 8, 9, 16, 17, 20, 118
forest, 11, 31, 42, 91, 117
fortress(es), 45
forty-eight, lower, 11, 31, 32, 34, 38–41
France, 63, 67–69, 73, 120
freedom(s), 76, 78, 85, 86
freighter(s), 63, 65

frieze(s), 102, 103, 111
frontier(s), 4–6, 8–12, 20, 24, 25, 31, 39, 41, 42, 47, 50, 56, 57, 68, 69, 82, 95
Fuji(yama), Mount, 88, 91–93, 95
funeral(s), 38

Galilee, Sea of, 15, 16, 67
gallery, 117
Gandhi, Mahatma, 84
Ganesh, 112
genius, human, 97, 101
Germany, 120, 121, 125
Gershwin, George, 125
    Porgy and Bess, 125
ghat(s), 80
Gibraltar, 68
Gihon spring, 113
Ginza, 91
globe, 47, 91, 121, 129
goal, 36, 38
God, 77, 89, 98, 99, 101, 112, 113
god(dess)(es), 97, 102, 105, 107, 109, 111, 112, 114, 117
gold rush, 11
golden triangle, 23
Good Neighbor Policy, 44
good(ness), 59, 84, 102, 128, 129
goods, 44, 52, 53, 119
goodwill, 126
Gopini(s) (milkmaids), 117
Grand Canyon, 114
Great Basin, 93
Great Britain, 1, 18, 52, 125. *See also* England
Great Pyramid, 102
Greece, 5, 8, 21, 102, 103, 106, 120
guide(s), 2, 17, 63, 91, 92, 101, 102, 106, 123
    Intourist, 20, 21, 29, 46, 127
    Israeli, 68
Gulf of Mexico, 65
gun(s), 10, 16, 29, 56, 68, 69, 72
Hadith, 77
Haines Cutoff, 11, 12

Halliburton, Richard, 88, 89, 91
happiness, 79, 80, 84, 85, 127–129
harbor(s), 31, 63
hardship(s), 45
harmony, biblical, 16
"Heart of the Andes" (Church), 90
Helena, 13
Hephaestus, 102,
heritage, 72, 75, 97, 103–105, 116
Her Majesty's Mail Service, 12
Hermitage, 18
hero, 12
Hezekiah's Tunnel, 47, 113, 114
highway(s), 11, 26, 43, 44, 47, 53, 76
    interstate, 52, 53
hijab, 76
hik(e)(ing), 1, 9, 14, 35, 36, 45, 107
Himalayan passes, 48
Hindu Kush Mountains, 47, 95
Hindu(ism)(s), 78, 82, 84, 104, 105, 111, 112, 117
history, 36, 47, 48, 52, 79, 97, 103, 115, 127
    natural, 62
hitchhiking (auto stopping), 2
Hitching Post of the Sun. *See* Intihuatana stone
holds, ship, 32, 33, 60
    segregated, 61
Holy Land, 1, 4, 8, 14
Homer, 8, 30
Hong Kong, 22, 91
honor, 73
Hopi reservation, 25, 28
Hopis, 26
horizon, 35, 58, 83
hostel(s), 2, 17, 70, 99, 125, 126
house arrest, 21, 23, 27
Hudson River, 51, 52
human being(s), 42, 84, 87, 90, 97–100, 102, 105, 116
human(ity)(kind)(race), 42, 47, 49, 55, 97, 99, 102, 110, 114, 128, 129
husband(s), 33, 40, 42, 73, 77, 80, 81, 85

Ibrahim. *See* Abraham

ice break up/freeze up, 31, 32
idea(s), 1, 2, 55, 79
identity, 9, 29, 48, 102
  mistaken, 4, 25
ignorance, 24, 80, 124, 126
Iguaçu Falls/River, 87, 88, 90, 93, 99
Illampu Peak, 90
Illiami Peak, 90
illusion, optical, 58
image(ry)(s), 98, 99, 105, 114, 117, 120
imagination, 3, 43, 46, 47, 53, 71, 106,
    108, 109, 115
Inca Trail, 107
inconsistenc(ies)(y), 25, 29, 130
independence, Algerian, 68, 71–74
India, 19, 31, 48, 57, 58, 71, 78, 82, 92,
    98, 99, 104, 117, 118, 121, 122
Indiana, 51
Indian River, 31
indigenous people(s), 26, 56, 114
Inter-American Highway, 43–46, 49
innovation(s), 63, 128
institution(s), 65
interpretation, 130
interrogation, 6, 15, 16, 24, 25
Intihuatana stone, 108
Inti Raymi, 108
Intourist USSR, 17–21, 29, 46, 54, 55,
    75, 104, 127
Inupiats, 26
Ireland, 125
Irrawaddy River, 22, 58, 59, 61
Islam, 46, 55, 69, 75, 76, 82–86
Israel(is), 1, 8, 11, 14, 16, 17, 47, 63,
    67, 112, 125
Israelites, 113
Italy, 4, 63, 99, 120, 121

jail, 16, 16, 23, 25, 26, 28, 29, 39
janitors, 55, 66
Japan, 18, 19, 22, 91, 92
Jefferson, Thomas, 79, 93
Jehan, Shah, 98, 99, 102
Jericho Ford, 67
Jerusalem, 15, 16, 23, 47, 112, 113

Jesus Christ, 14, 16, 67, 83, 112, 113
Jews, 10, 60, 63, 112, 113
Jordan(ians), 15, 17, 22, 28
Jordan River/Valley, 67, 68
Judaism, 55, 112, 113
judgment(s), 48, 94, 98, 130
jungle(s), 44, 58, 59, 109, 111
Jupiter, 112
justice, 53, 60, 66, 110, 113, 127–129
  injustice, 11

Kazakhstan, 75
KGB, 19, 20, 29
Khan, Kublai, 110
Khyber Pass, 19, 47, 48, 95
kibbutz(im), 63, 67
kilos, 5
kindness, 56, 60, 113
King of the Dark Chamber (Tagore), 125
Kipling, Rudyard, 57–59
  "Road to Mandalay," 57–59
knowledge, 2, 24, 29, 37, 42, 55, 80, 98,
    102, 104, 105, 111
Komsomol, 18
Krishna, Lord, 117
kuffiyeh, 77

labor(ers), 97, 98, 102
La Guaira, port of, 65
Lake of the Andes, 90, 94. *See also*
    Lake Titicaca
language, 2, 5, 19, 29, 36, 37, 73, 77,
    86, 91, 114, 115, 126
Latin America, 21, 24, 44, 52, 121
law(s), 16, 22, 29, 39, 64, 75, 80, 85
Lawrence of Arabia, 9
leaders, 37, 72, 105
life, 1, 64, 66, 88, 105, 111, 113, 117,
    129, 130
  abundance of, 42, 66, 83
  in Alaska, 35, 37, 40, 42, 44
  in harem, 79
  holy, 84
  loss of, 33, 98, 105, 115
  in lower forty-eight, 31

mistakes in, 68
Muslim, 76
next (after death), 59, 60, 85, 97
possible, 65
in Purdah, 80
ruled by religious custom, 82
satisfactory, 82
Soviet, 75
lifestyle (American way of), 32, 37, 41,
          42, 73, 128
liberty, 53, 55, 56
librar(ies)(y), 87, 95, 108
Libya, 78, 79, 82, 119
lie (lying), 6, 7, 15, 19, 24, 25, 28
Lord, the, 14. *See also* Jesus Christ
Lord of the Cosmic Dance, 118. *See
          also* Nataraja
Lost City of the Incas, 108. *See* Machu
          Picchu
Louisiana, 65
love, 82, 97, 99, 113, 116
Lynn Canal, 11

Macedonia, 5, 9
Machu Picchu, 45, 65, 107, 108
madraseh(s), 46
Mahal, Mumtaz, 98, 99
malefactor(s), 26
Mandelbaum Gate, 17
Maracaibo, Lake, 94
marriage(s), 75, 81, 82
Marshal, U.S., 13, 39, 40
mashhad, 113
mask(s), face, 72, 76, 77
Mazama, Mount, 95
Mecca, 76, 112, 113
megalith(s), 107
memor(ies)(y), 2–4, 17, 19, 21, 23, 25,
          33, 59, 67, 88, 93, 94, 108, 120,
          124, 125
     collective, 114
The Merchant of Venice (Shakespeare), 124
Meru, Mount, 111
Mesa Verde, 114
Mexico, 12, 43, 44, 65, 108

Middle Ages, 46
military, the, 20
milkmaid(s), 117
minaret(s), 55
minorit(ies)(y), 13, 37, 65, 73, 128
Mississippi River, 51
Missouri, 51
Missouri River, 61
modernity, 80, 108
modesty, 77, 78, 85, 86, 126
Mohammed, 77, 85, 112
monogamy, 75
mood, 29, 46, 77
moon, full, 88, 99
moonlight, 46, 47, 88, 99
Moore, Sir Thomas, 80
morals, 6
moral weighing, 19
Moriah, Mount, 112, 113
Morocco, 68
Moses, 112
moshav(*im*), 67, 68
mosques, 46, 47, 54, 55, 75, 76, 98, 113
motiv(ation)(e)(s), 17, 24, 105, 116
Moulmein pagoda, 58
Mount Quarantania, 14
Mount of Temptation, 13, 14
mountain(s), 4, 14, 15, 22, 31, 44, 45,
          47–49, 56, 90–93, 112, 117
Mounted Police, Royal Canadian, 12,
          13, 30
Mountie(s), Canadian, 12, 13
Mughal Empire, 98
Muslim countr(ies)(y)/world, 49, 55,
          59, 69, 75, 77, 80, 82, 83, 85,
          86, 113, 119
Muslims, 77, 78, 83, 84, 112, 113
Myanmar (Burma), 21–23, 27, 58, 59,
          109, 110, 121

Nataraja, 118
nations, faults of, 1, 66, 103, 116, 127, 129
native tongue, 2, 36
Nativity, 16
Navajos, 26, 114

naval base(s), 31, 65
Nebuchadrezzar II, 112
the Netherlands, 1, 120
New York City, 1, 27, 100, 102, 104
New Zealand, 2, 125
Nile River, 60, 68
Nirvana, 60
Nobel Laureate, 125
North America, 114
north, far, 41, 44
North Star, 32
Norway, 127
Nubian pyramids, 93

observator(ies)(y), 107, 108
officer(s), 3, 6, 22–24, 26, 30, 31, 48, 60
official(s), 3, 6, 8, 16, 21, 22, 24, 25, 43, 48, 57, 69, 72, 77, 101, 104
Ohio River, 61
Old Roman Road, 47
Old Silk Road, 46, 47, 52
Oregon, 95
orientation (directional, spatial), 21, 36
Orient Express, 5, 53, 56
Ottoman Empire, 103

P&O Cruise Line, 23
Pacha Unachaq, 108
pagoda(s), 58, 109–111
painting(s), 90, 98, 104
Pakistan, 47–49, 76–78, 84–86, 95, 122
Palestine, 1, 13, 15
Pamulkale, 89, 90, 99
Panama, 43, 44
Panama Canal, 43
Pan-American Highway, 43, 44
Panhandle of Alaska, 39
Parthenon, 102–104, 116
Parvati, 117
Paso del condor, 48, 49, 56, 90, 94
pass(es), mountain, 47–49, 90
passport, 13, 15–17, 22–24, 26, 27, 30, 57
Paul the Apostle, 89
Peace Corps, U.S., 45

peer(s), 7, 8
pension(s), 8, 17
perception(s), 2, 16, 86, 130
Persia, 112, 113
Peru, 44, 45, 107, 123
phallic symbol(s), 117
Phoenicians, 109
photographs(s), 89, 90, 94
pilgrim(age)(s), 1, 13, 16, 17, 47, 67, 89, 113
Pioneer Palace, 17, 18
pipeline, trans-Alaskan, 43
police, 3, 4, 6–8, 10, 12–17, 19, 21–30, 39, 79
Politburo, 20
political order, 1
Polo, Marco, 46
polygamy, 75, 83
Pompey, 112
Porgy and Bess (Gershwin), 125
port(s), 23, 33, 59, 63–65, 83
poverty, 56, 65
Powers, Gary Francis, 19
Pravda, 17
pre-Columbian peoples, 108, 109
priest(s), 106–109
problems, 1, 52, 64, 73, 116, 128, 129
Promised Land, 13, 63
propaganda, 55
property, 79
protection, 77
provider, good, 40, 81
Provisional Government, Algerian, 69
psyche, 6, 79
Public Health Service, United States, 31
Puerto Rico, 3, 58
purdah, 78–82, 86
purifying tablets, 125
Pyramid of the Moon, 109
pyramids, 93, 97, 101, 102, 105, 106, 109

Quarantania, Mount, 14
Qu'ran, 46, 76, 77, 82, 83, 112
racism, 64, 128
railroad(s), 19, 21, 53, 56, 65, 68, 71

Alaskan, 35
Siberian, 18
Ramadan, 83–85
reality, 2, 14, 26, 64, 107, 130
Red China, 2
reflex, 19, 68
reform(s), 76
refugee(s), 63
regimes, Mogul, 105
regret(s), 27, 68, 87, 102, 118
religion(s), 14, 55, 60, 76, 82, 84, 105,
        108, 111, 128
    Buddhist, 104, 110
    Islamic, 75
    Orthodox, 75
replica(s), 98, 103, 116
reservation(s), 25, 26, 28, 115, 123
reservoirs, 100
resources, 37, 94
restoration(s), 103, 106, 114, 116
retreat, religious, 7, 8
Revelation(s), 89
Revillagigedo Channel/Rock, 33
revolt(s), 127
Richardson Highway, 43
rifle(s), 6, 10, 22, 23, 29, 67, 68, 71–74
right(s), 113, 128
Rio Grande River, 118
Rio Madeira, 50, 61, 62
risk(s), 2, 38, 97
rituals, pagan, 107
rivers, 4, 14, 44, 51, 62, 63, 65, 109, 111
riverboat(s), 23, 58, 59
road(s), 3, 43–53, 65, 68, 92, 121
    non-roads, 49–51
    riverine, 59, 61, 63
    U.S., 52
roadhouse(s), 11, 12
"Road to Mandalay" (Kipling), 57, 59
Rocky Mountains, 61
Roman legions, 47
Romans, 102, 112, 113, 122
Rome, 106, 127
Roosevelt, Franklin Delano, 44, 85
rubles, 21, 54

ruin(s), 15, 45–48, 54, 110, 111, 114
Rushmore, Mount, 105
Russia(ns), 18, 19, 21, 32
Russian Orthodox Church, 38, 55

Sabbath, 63
sacredness, 91
Sahara Desert, 68
samovar, 53, 54
scenery, 35, 60
school(s), 69, 70
    Muslim, 75, 76, 81, 82
    Qu'anic, 46
    South American, 123, 124
    third-world, 124
Scotty Creek, 11
Scythopolis, 67
sea level, 47, 48
Sea of Galilee, 15, 16, 67
sea lane(s), 57, 59, 63
Seattle-Alaska connection, 41
self-deception, 36
self-perception, 28, 29, 126, 130
sense(s), 94, 95
sepoys, 48
sequoias, giant (Big Trees), 93
serendipity, 89, 96, 99
sermons in stone, 117
sex(uality), 10, 83, 85, 99, 126
Shakespeare, William, 124
    The Merchant of Venice, 124
Shangri-la, 1, 23
shelter(s), 10, 22, 23, 57, 59, 84, 101
ship(s), 18, 23, 32, 33, 44, 57, 59, 60,
        63, 64, 83, 84, 109
Shiva linga, 117, 118
shrine(s), 109, 111, 113
Siberia, 19
"Silence implies consent," 80
Sinai, Mount, 112
Sioux reservation, 123
Sitka Sound, 31
slavery, 103, 116
soap, 6
social engineering, 1

society, 1, 38, 125, 127–129
soldier(s), 10, 22, 23, 29, 71, 78, 86
solidarity, 97
Somename, Lord, 7
souk (bazaar), 69
South Africa, 125
South America, 44, 45, 56, 61, 66, 89,
    94, 126
Soviet Union/USSR (Empire), 17, 19–
    21, 23, 41, 46, 52–55, 68, 75,
    80, 124, 127
space programs, 20
Spain, 68
S.S. United States, 1, 63, 64
Star and Crescent, 69, 73
star route, 12, 26
statehood, Alaskan, 42
steerage, 2, 60–62
steppe(s), 55, 76
Stonehenge, 93, 105–109
Stratford-upon-Avon, 124
stress, 82, 85, 86
stupa(s), 109, 110
subjugation of women, 103, 116
Sudan, 49, 60, 61, 68
Suez Canal, 67
suffrage, 76
sultan(s), 9, 47, 112
sunrise, 4, 28, 58, 83, 84, 107, 108
survival, 28, 42, 113, 114
Susitna, 32–34
Sweden, 128
symbol(ism)(s), 69, 72, 77, 82, 110,
    112, 117, 129, 130
Syria, 8–10, 15, 68

Tagore, Rabindranath, 125
   King of the Dark Chamber, 125
Taj Mahal, 98, 102–105, 110, 116
Tajikistan, 75
Tashkent Express, 20, 53, 56
tax, income, 54, 123, 124
technology, 42, 98, 101, 108, 114, 128,
    129, 130

temple(s), 103–105, 107, 109, 111–113,
    117
Temptation of Christ, 14
terror, 16, 29, 67, 71, 74
terrorists, 86, 101
Texas, 44, 46
Thailand, 22, 23, 58
third class, 2, 19, 53–57, 63
Third Mesa, 25
Thlingits, 26, 36
Titicaca, Lake, 90, 93, 94
tomb(s), 98, 106
trading post(s), 11, 38
tradition(s), 14, 49, 77, 120
   Arab, 77
   Buddhist/Hindu, 58, 111
   Christian, 60
   European, 125
   Greek, 103
   Islamic, 75
   Japanese, 92
   Judaic, 60, 112
train(s), 5–7, 11, 18–23, 35, 53–58, 61,
    64, 69–71, 90–92, 107
translation, 104
transportation, 11, 57
Trans-Siberian Railroad, 18
trappers, 12
travelers checks, 4, 7, 23, 69, 70
triumphalism, 112
troops, 53
tropics, 58
trust, 85
truth, 2, 40, 55, 111
tundra, 36, 42
Turkey, 8–10, 27, 45, 68, 76, 83, 89,
    103
Turkish empire, 9
Turks, 8, 9

ultimate(s) (places), 36
UNESCO, 87
United Kingdom, 121
United States, 1, 3, 5, 6, 12, 13, 16, 17,
    19, 21, 24–26, 28, 31, 36, 43,

44, 51–53, 58, 56, 59, 63–66,
   75, 77, 78, 82, 86, 114, 119,
   121–130
universe, 92, 107, 111, 112, 118
Ural Mountains, 55, 112
Urdu, 77
Urubamba Gorge, 108
US Routes (1, 9, and 40), 3, 51, 52
Utah, 75
Uzbekistan, 46, 55, 75

values, 6, 17, 28–30, 66, 74, 76, 86,
   115, 116, 126–130
value system, 6, 28
veil(s), 72, 74–78, 85
vendor(s), 118
Venezuela, 24, 65, 94
Victoria Falls, 95
Viet Nam, 21
vihara(s), Buddhist, 121
Virginia, 64, 127
visa(s), 9, 20, 62, 69, 91–93
void, formless, 118
volcano(s), 31, 95
voyage(s), 64, 65, 85

Wales, Lake, 57
war, 9, 48, 53, 67–74, 113, 126, 127
   Algerian, 73
   1956 Israeli, 11
   Six-Day Israeli, 11
   Suez War, 8
   World War II, 9, 11, 31, 52, 125
warfare, gorilla, 68, 72
Washington (state), 33
water, drinkable, 6–8, 12, 14, 15, 45, 50,
   83, 84, 100–102, 111, 114, 118
   purified, 123
   weapons, 16
Western Sea, 46. *See* also Pacific Ocean
Western Wall, 112, 113
White Pass, 11
wi(fe)(ves), 22, 40, 49, 78–83, 85, 86, 98
Wien Airline, 32, 35, 40
willow-ware china, 92

wisdom, 73, 115
women, 60
   American, 24, 25
   Mestizo, 24
   Muslim, 72, 76–78, 80–86, 119
   Russian, 21
   segregation from men of, 49, 75
   subjugation of, 103, 116
   Western, 85
wonder(s), 1
   built, 27, 97–116
   natural, 87–96
word of God, 77
words, triple-letter, 114, 115
Wordsworth, William, 110
work, 18, 40, 66, 78, 79, 85, 97, 101,
   105, 110
workers, 45, 65, 100, 101, 105, 106, 115
   Egyptian, 101
   social, 63
work ethic, 124
works, good, 105
World Heritage Sites, UNESCO, 87
worship, 98, 106, 110, 112, 113, 117

Yahweh, 113
Yankee(s), 7, 8, 19, 45, 65
yoni, 117
Young Pioneers, Soviet, 17, 18
Yugoslavia, 4–6, 8
Yukon River/Territory, 11, 12, 38, 43

Zaccheus' tree, 13, 28
Zakat, 60
Zambia, 95
Zimbabwe (Rhodesia), 95

VIBS

The **Value Inquiry Book Series** is co-sponsored by:

Adler School of Professional Psychology
American Indian Philosophy Association
American Maritain Association
American Society for Value Inquiry
Association for Process Philosophy of Education
Canadian Society for Philosophical Practice
Center for Bioethics, University of Turku
Center for Professional and Applied Ethics, University of North Carolina at Charlotte
Central European Pragmatist Forum
Centre for Applied Ethics, Hong Kong Baptist University
Centre for Cultural Research, Aarhus University
Centre for Professional Ethics, University of Central Lancashire
Centre for the Study of Philosophy and Religion, University College of Cape Breton
Centro de Estudos em Filosofia Americana, Brazil
College of Education and Allied Professions, Bowling Green State University
College of Liberal Arts, Rochester Institute of Technology
Concerned Philosophers for Peace
Conference of Philosophical Societies
Department of Moral and Social Philosophy, University of Helsinki
Gannon University
Gilson Society
Haitian Studies Association
Ikeda University
Institute of Philosophy of the High Council of Scientific Research, Spain
International Academy of Philosophy of the Principality of Liechtenstein
International Association of Bioethics
International Center for the Arts, Humanities, and Value Inquiry
International Society for Universal Dialogue
Natural Law Society
Philosophical Society of Finland
Philosophy Born of Struggle Association
Philosophy Seminar, University of Mainz
Pragmatism Archive at The Oklahoma State University
R.S. Hartman Institute for Formal and Applied Axiology
Research Institute, Lakeridge Health Corporation
Russian Philosophical Society
Society for Existential Analysis
Society for Iberian and Latin-American Thought
Society for the Philosophic Study of Genocide and the Holocaust
Unit for Research in Cognitive Neuroscience, Autonomous University of Barcelona
Yves R. Simon Institute

Titles Published

1. Noel Balzer, *The Human Being as a Logical Thinker*

2. Archie J. Bahm, *Axiology: The Science of Values*

3. H. P. P. (Hennie) Lötter, *Justice for an Unjust Society*

4. H. G. Callaway, *Context for Meaning and Analysis: A Critical Study in the Philosophy of Language*

5. Benjamin S. Llamzon, *A Humane Case for Moral Intuition*

6. James R. Watson, *Between Auschwitz and Tradition: Postmodern Reflections on the Task of Thinking.* A volume in **Holocaust and Genocide Studies**

7. Robert S. Hartman, *Freedom to Live: The Robert Hartman Story*, Edited by Arthur R. Ellis. A volume in **Hartman Institute Axiology Studies**

8. Archie J. Bahm, *Ethics: The Science of Oughtness*

9. George David Miller, *An Idiosyncratic Ethics; Or, the Lauramachean Ethics*

10. Joseph P. DeMarco, *A Coherence Theory in Ethics*

11. Frank G. Forrest, *Valuemetrics^x: The Science of Personal and Professional Ethics.* A volume in **Hartman Institute Axiology Studies**

12. William Gerber, *The Meaning of Life: Insights of the World's Great Thinkers*

13. Richard T. Hull, Editor, *A Quarter Century of Value Inquiry: Presidential Addresses of the American Society for Value Inquiry.* A volume in **Histories and Addresses of Philosophical Societies**

14. William Gerber, *Nuggets of Wisdom from Great Jewish Thinkers: From Biblical Times to the Present*

15. Sidney Axinn, *The Logic of Hope: Extensions of Kant's View of Religion*

16. Messay Kebede, *Meaning and Development*

17. Amihud Gilead, *The Platonic Odyssey: A Philosophical-Literary Inquiry into the Phaedo*

18. Necip Fikri Alican, *Mill's Principle of Utility: A Defense of John Stuart Mill's Notorious Proof.* A volume in **Universal Justice**

19. Michael H. Mitias, Editor, *Philosophy and Architecture.*

20. Roger T. Simonds, *Rational Individualism: The Perennial Philosophy of Legal Interpretation.* A volume in **Natural Law Studies**

21. William Pencak, The Conflict of Law and Justice in the Icelandic Sagas

22. Samuel M. Natale and Brian M. Rothschild, Editors, *Values, Work, Education: The Meanings of Work*

23. N. Georgopoulos and Michael Heim, Editors, *Being Human in the Ultimate: Studies in the Thought of John M. Anderson*

24. Robert Wesson and Patricia A. Williams, Editors, *Evolution and Human Values*

25. Wim J. van der Steen, *Facts, Values, and Methodology: A New Approach to Ethics*

26. Avi Sagi and Daniel Statman, *Religion and Morality*

27. Albert William Levi, *The High Road of Humanity: The Seven Ethical Ages of Western Man*, Edited by Donald Phillip Verene and Molly Black Verene

28. Samuel M. Natale and Brian M. Rothschild, Editors, *Work Values: Education, Organization, and Religious Concerns*

29. Laurence F. Bove and Laura Duhan Kaplan, Editors, *From the Eye of the Storm: Regional Conflicts and the Philosophy of Peace*. A volume in **Philosophy of Peace**

30. Robin Attfield, *Value, Obligation, and Meta-Ethics*

31.   William Gerber, *The Deepest Questions You Can Ask About God: As Answered by the World's Great Thinkers*

32.   Daniel Statman, *Moral Dilemmas*

33.   Rem B. Edwards, Editor, *Formal Axiology and Its Critics*. A volume in **Hartman Institute Axiology Studies**

34.   George David Miller and Conrad P. Pritscher, *On Education and Values: In Praise of Pariahs and Nomads*. A volume in **Philosophy of Education**

35.   Paul S. Penner, *Altruistic Behavior: An Inquiry into Motivation*

36.   Corbin Fowler, *Morality for Moderns*

37.   Giambattista Vico, *The Art of Rhetoric* (*Institutiones Oratoriae*, 1711–1741), from the definitive Latin text and notes, Italian commentary and introduction byGiuliano Crifò.Translated and Edited by Giorgio A. Pinton and Arthur W. Shippee. A volume in **Values in Italian Philosophy**

38.   W. H. Werkmeister, *Martin Heidegger on the Way*. Edited by Richard T. Hull. A volume in **Werkmeister Studies**

39.   Phillip Stambovsky, *Myth and the Limits of Reason*

40.   Samantha Brennan, Tracy Isaacs, and Michael Milde, Editors, *A Question of Values: New Canadian Perspectives in Ethics and Political Philosophy*

41.   Peter A. Redpath, *Cartesian Nightmare: An Introduction to Transcendental Sophistry*. A volume in **Studies in the History of Western Philosophy**

42.   Clark Butler, *History as the Story of Freedom: Philosophy in InterculturalContext*, with responses by sixteen scholars

43.   Dennis Rohatyn, *Philosophy History Sophistry*

44.   Leon Shaskolsky Sheleff, *Social Cohesion and Legal Coercion: A Critique of Weber, Durkheim, and Marx*. Afterword by Virginia Black

45.   Alan Soble, Editor, *Sex, Love, and Friendship: Studies of the Society for the Philosophy of Sex and Love, 1977–1992*. A volume in **Histories and Addresses of Philosophical Societies**

46. Peter A. Redpath, *Wisdom's Odyssey: From Philosophy to Transcendental Sophistry.* A volume in **Studies in the History of Western Philosophy**

47. Albert A. Anderson, *Universal Justice: A Dialectical Approach.* A volume in **Universal Justice**

48. Pio Colonnello, *The Philosophy of José Gaos.* Translated from Italian by Peter Cocozzella. Edited by Myra Moss. Introduction by Giovanni Gullace. A volume in **Values in Italian Philosophy**

49. Laura Duhan Kaplan and Laurence F. Bove, Editors, *Philosophical Perspectives on Power and Domination: Theories and Practices.* A volume in **Philosophy of Peace**

50. Gregory F. Mellema, *Collective Responsibility*

51. Josef Seifert, *What Is Life? The Originality, Irreducibility, and Value of Life.* A volume in **Central-European Value Studies**

52. William Gerber, *Anatomy of What We Value Most*

53. Armando Molina, *Our Ways: Values and Character*, Edited by Rem B. Edwards. A volume in **Hartman Institute Axiology Studies**

54. Kathleen J. Wininger, *Nietzsche's Reclamation of Philosophy.* A volume in **Central-European Value Studies**

55. Thomas Magnell, Editor, *Explorations of Value*

56. HPP (Hennie) Lötter, *Injustice, Violence, and Peace: The Case of South Africa.* A volume in **Philosophy of Peace**

57. Lennart Nordenfelt, *Talking About Health: A Philosophical Dialogue.* A volume in **Nordic Value Studies**

58. Jon Mills and Janusz A. Polanowski, *The Ontology of Prejudice.* A volume in **Philosophy and Psychology**

59. Leena Vilkka, *The Intrinsic Value of Nature*

60. Palmer Talbutt, Jr., Rough Dialectics: *Sorokin's Philosophy of Value*, with contributions by Lawrence T. Nichols and Pitirim A. Sorokin

61. C. L. Sheng, *A Utilitarian General Theory of Value*

62. George David Miller, *Negotiating Toward Truth: The Extinction of Teachers and Students*. Epilogue by Mark Roelof Eleveld. A volume in **Philosophy of Education**

63. William Gerber, *Love, Poetry, and Immortality: Luminous Insights of the World's Great Thinkers*

64. Dane R. Gordon, Editor, *Philosophy in Post-Communist Europe*. A volume in **Post-Communist European Thought**

65. Dane R. Gordon and Józef Niznik, Editors, *Criticism and Defense of Rationality in Contemporary Philosophy*. A volume in **Post-Communist European Thought**

66. John R. Shook, *Pragmatism: An Annotated Bibliography, 1898-1940*. With contributions by E. Paul Colella, Lesley Friedman, Frank X. Ryan, and Ignas K. Skrupskelis

67. Lansana Keita, *The Human Project and the Temptations of Science*

68. Michael M. Kazanjian, *Phenomenology and Education: Cosmology, Co-Being, and Core Curriculum*. A volume in **Philosophy of Education**

69. James W. Vice, *The Reopening of the American Mind: On Skepticism and Constitutionalism*

70. Sarah Bishop Merrill, *Defining Personhood: Toward the Ethics of Quality in Clinical Care*

71. Dane R. Gordon, *Philosophy and Vision*

72. Alan Milchman and Alan Rosenberg, Editors, *Postmodernism and the Holocaust*. A volume in **Holocaust and Genocide Studies**

73. Peter A. Redpath, *Masquerade of the Dream Walkers: Prophetic Theology from the Cartesians to Hegel*. A volume in **Studies in the History of Western Philosophy**

74. Malcolm D. Evans, *Whitehead and Philosophy of Education: The Seamless Coat of Learning*. A volume in **Philosophy of Education**

75. Warren E. Steinkraus, *Taking Religious Claims Seriously: A Philosophy of Religion*, Edited by Michael H. Mitias. A volume in **Universal Justice**

76. Thomas Magnell, Editor, *Values and Education*

77. Kenneth A. Bryson, *Persons and Immortality*. A volume in **Natural Law Studies**

78. Steven V. Hicks, *International Law and the Possibility of a Just World Order: An Essay on Hegel's Universalism*. A volume in **Universal Justice**

79. E. F. Kaelin, *Texts on Texts and Textuality: A Phenomenology of Literary Art*, Edited by Ellen J. Burns

80. Amihud Gilead, *Saving Possibilities: A Study in Philosophical Psychology*. A volume in Philosophy and Psychology

81. André Mineau, *The Making of the Holocaust: Ideology and Ethics in the Systems Perspective*. A volume in **Holocaust and Genocide Studies**

82. Howard P. Kainz, *Politically Incorrect Dialogues: Topics Not Discussed in Polite Circles*

83. Veikko Launis, Juhani Pietarinen, and Juha Räikkä, Editors, *Genes and Morality: New Essays*. A volume in **Nordic Value Studies**

84. Steven Schroeder, *The Metaphysics of Cooperation: A Study of F. D. Maurice*

85. Caroline Joan ("Kay") S. Picart, *Thomas Mann and Friedrich Nietzsche: Eroticism, Death, Music, and Laughter*. A volume in **Central-European Value Studies**

86. G. John M. Abbarno, Editor, *The Ethics of Homelessness: Philosophical Perspectives*

87. James Giles, Editor, *French Existentialism: Consciousness, Ethics, and Relations with Others*. A volume in **Nordic Value Studies**

88. Deane Curtin and Robert Litke, Editors, *Institutional Violence*. A volume in **Philosophy of Peace**

89.   Yuval Lurie, *Cultural Beings: Reading the Philosophers of Genesis*

90.   Sandra A. Wawrytko, Editor, *The Problem of Evil: An Intercultural Exploration*. A volume in **Philosophy and Psychology**

91.   Gary J. Acquaviva, *Values, Violence, and Our Future*. A volume in **Hartman Institute Axiology Studies**

92.   Michael R. Rhodes, *Coercion: A Nonevaluative Approach*

93.   Jacques Kriel, *Matter, Mind, and Medicine: Transforming the Clinical Method*

94.   Haim Gordon, *Dwelling Poetically: Educational Challenges in Heidegger's Thinking on Poetry*. A volume in **Philosophy of Education**

95.   Ludwig Grünberg, *The Mystery of Values: Studies in Axiology*, Edited by Cornelia Grünberg and Laura Grünberg

96.   Gerhold K. Becker, Editor, *The Moral Status of Persons: Perspectives on Bioethics*. A volume in **Studies in Applied Ethics**

97.   Roxanne Claire Farrar, *Sartrean Dialectics: A Method for Critical Discourse on Aesthetic Experience*

98.   Ugo Spirito, *Memoirs of the Twentieth Century*. Translated from Italian and Edited by Anthony G. Costantini. A volume in **Values in Italian Philosophy**

99.   Steven Schroeder, *Between Freedom and Necessity: An Essay on the Place of Value*

100.   Foster N. Walker, *Enjoyment and the Activity of Mind: Dialogues on Whitehead and Education*. A volume in **Philosophy of Education**

101.   Avi Sagi, Kierkegaard, *Religion, and Existence: The Voyage of the Self*. Translated from Hebrew by Batya Stein

102.   Bennie R. Crockett, Jr., Editor, *Addresses of the Mississippi Philosophical Association*. A volume in **Histories and Addresses of Philosophical Societies**

103.   Paul van Dijk, *Anthropology in the Age of Technology: The Philosophical Contribution of Günther Anders*

104.   Giambattista Vico, *Universal Right*. Translated from Latin and edited by Giorgio Pinton and Margaret Diehl. A volume in **Values in Italian Philosophy**

105.   Judith Presler and Sally J. Scholz, Editors, *Peacemaking: Lessons from the Past, Visions for the Future*. A volume in **Philosophy of Peace**

106.   Dennis Bonnette, *Origin of the Human Species*. A volume in **Studies in the History of Western Philosophy**

107.   Phyllis Chiasson, *Peirce's Pragmatism: The Design for Thinking*. A volume in **Studies in Pragmatism and Values**

108.   Dan Stone, Editor, *Theoretical Interpretations of the Hol*ocaust. A volume in **Holocaust and Genocide Studies**

109.   Raymond Angelo Belliotti, *What Is the Meaning of Human Life?*

110.   Lennart Nordenfelt, *Health, Science, and Ordinary Language*, with Contributions by George Khushf and K. W. M. Fulford

111.   Daryl Koehn, *Local Insights, Global Ethics for Business*. A volume in **Studies in Applied Ethics**

112.   Matti Häyry and Tuija Takala, Editors, *The Future of Value Inquiry*. A volume in **Nordic Value Studies**

113.   Conrad P. Pritscher, *Quantum Learning: Beyond Duality*

114.   Thomas M. Dicken and Rem B. Edwards, *Dialogues on Values and Centers of Value: Old Friends, New Thoughts*. A volume in **Hartman Institute Axiology Studies**

115.   Rem B. Edwards, *What Caused the Big Bang?* A volume in **Philosophy and Religion**

116.   Jon Mills, Editor, *A Pedagogy of Becoming*. A volume in **Philosophy of Education**

117. Robert T. Radford, *Cicero: A Study in the Origins of Republican Philosophy*. A volume in **Studies in the History of Western Philosophy**

118. Arleen L. F. Salles and María Julia Bertomeu, Editors, *Bioethics: Latin American Perspectives*. A volume in **Philosophy in Latin America**

119. Nicola Abbagnano, *The Human Project: The Year 2000*, with an Interview by Guiseppe Grieco. Translated from Italian by Bruno Martini and Nino Langiulli. Edited with an introduction by Nino Langiulli. A volume in **Studies in the History of Western Philosophy**

120. Daniel M. Haybron, Editor, *Earth's Abominations: Philosophical Studies of Evil*. A volume in **Personalist Studies**

121. Anna T. Challenger, *Philosophy and Art in Gurdjieff's* Beelzebub: *A Modern Sufi Odyssey*

122. George David Miller, *Peace, Value, and Wisdom: The Educational Philosophy of Daisaku Ikeda*. A volume in **Daisaku Ikeda Studies**

123. Haim Gordon and Rivca Gordon, *Sophistry and Twentieth-Century Art*

124. Thomas O. Buford and Harold H. Oliver, Editors *Personalism Revisited: Its Proponents and Critics*. A volume in **Histories and Addresses of Philosophical Societies**

125. Avi Sagi, *Albert Camus and the Philosophy of the Absurd*. Translated from Hebrew by Batya Stein

126. Robert S. Hartman, *The Knowledge of Good: Critique of Axiological Reason*. Expanded translation from the Spanish by Robert S. Hartman. Edited by Arthur R. Ellis and Rem B. Edwards.A volume in **Hartman Institute Axiology Studies**

127. Alison Bailey and Paula J. Smithka, Editors. *Community, Diversity, and Difference: Implications for Peace*. A volume in **Philosophy of Peace**

128. Oscar Vilarroya, *The Dissolution of Mind: A Fable of How Experience Gives Rise to Cognition*. A volume in **Cognitive Science**

129. Paul Custodio Bube and Jeffery Geller, Editors, *Conversations with Pragmatism: A Multi-Disciplinary Study*. A volume in **Studies in Pragmatism and Values**

130.　Richard Rumana, *Richard Rorty: An Annotated Bibliography of Secondary Literature*. A volume in **Studies in Pragmatism and Values**

131.　Stephen Schneck, Editor, *Max Scheler's Acting Persons: New Perspectives* A volume in **Personalist Studies**

132.　Michael Kazanjian, *Learning Values Lifelong: From Inert Ideas to Wholes*. A volume in **Philosophy of Education**

133.　Rudolph Alexander Kofi Cain, Alain Leroy Locke: *Race, Culture, and the Education of African American Adults*. A volume in **African American Philosophy**

134.　Werner Krieglstein, *Compassion: A New Philosophy of the Other*

135.　Robert N. Fisher, Daniel T. Primozic, Peter A. Day, and Joel A. Thompson, Editors, *Suffering, Death, and Identity*. A volume in **Personalist Studies**

136.　Steven Schroeder, *Touching Philosophy, Sounding Religion, Placing Education*. A volume in **Philosophy of Education**

137.　Guy DeBrock, *Process Pragmatism: Essays on a Quiet Philosophical Revolution*. A volume in **Studies in Pragmatism and Values**

138.　Lennart Nordenfelt and Per-Erik Liss, Editors, *Dimensions of Health and Health Promotion*

139.　Amihud Gilead, *Singularity and Other Possibilities: Panenmentalist Novelties*

140.　Samantha Mei-che Pang, *Nursing Ethics in Modern China: Conflicting Values and Competing Role Requirements*. A volume in **Studies in Applied Ethics**

141.　Christine M. Koggel, Allannah Furlong, and Charles Levin, Editors, *Confidential Relationships: Psychoanalytic, Ethical, and Legal Contexts*. A volume in **Philosophy and Psychology**

142.　Peter A. Redpath, Editor, *A Thomistic Tapestry: Essays in Memory of Étienne Gilson*. A volume in **Gilson Studies**

143.   Deane-Peter Baker and Patrick Maxwell, Editors, *Explorations in Contemporary Continental Philosophy of Religion*. A volume in **Philosophy and Religion**

144.   Matti Häyry and Tuija Takala, Editors, *Scratching the Surface of Bioethics*. A volume in **Values in Bioethics**

145.   Leonidas Donskis, *Forms of Hatred: The Troubled Imagination in Modern Philosophy and Literature*

146.   Andreea Deciu Ritivoi, Editor, *Interpretation and Its Objects: Studies in the Philosophy of Michael Krausz*

147.   Herman Stark, *A Fierce Little Tragedy: Thought, Passion, and Self-Formation in the Philosophy Classroom*. A volume in **Philosophy of Education**

148.   William Gay and Tatiana Alekseeva, Editors, *Democracy and the Quest for Justice: Russian and American Perspectives*. A volume in **Contemporary Russian Philosophy**

149.   Xunwu Chen, *Being and Authenticity*

150.   Hugh P. McDonald, *Radical Axiology: A First Philosophy of Values*

151.   Dane R. Gordon and David C. Durst, Editors, *Civil Society in Southeast Europe*. A volume in **Post-Communist European Thought**

152.   John Ryder and Emil Višňovský, Editors, *Pragmatism and Values: The Central European Pragmatist Forum, Volume One*. A volume in **Studies in Pragmatism and Values**

153.   Messay Kebede, *Africa's Quest for a Philosophy of Decolonization*

154.   Steven M. Rosen, *Dimensions of* Apeiron: *A Topological Phenomenology of Space, Time, and Individuation*. A volume in **Philosophy and Psychology**

155.   Albert A. Anderson, Steven V. Hicks, and Lech Witkowski, Editors, *Mythos and Logos: How to Regain the Love of Wisdom*. A volume in **Universal Justice**

156.   John Ryder and Krystyna Wilkoszewska, Editors, *Deconstruction and Reconstruction: The Central European Pragmatist Forum, Volume Two*. A volume in **Studies in Pragmatism and Values**

157.   Javier Muguerza, *Ethics and Perplexity: Toward a Critique of Dialogical Reason*. Translated from the Spanish by Jody L. Doran. Edited by John R. Welch. A volume in **Philosophy in Spain**

158.   Gregory F. Mellema, *The Expectations of Morality*

159.   Robert Ginsberg, *The Aesthetics of Ruins*

160.   Stan van Hooft, *Life, Death, and Subjectivity: Moral Sources in Bioethics* A volume in **Values in Bioethics**

161.   André Mineau, *Operation Barbarossa: Ideology and Ethics Against Human Dignity*

162.   Arthur Efron, *Expriencing Tess of the D'Urbervilles: A Deweyan Account.* A volume in **Studies in Pragmatism and Values**

163.   Reyes Mate, *Memory of the West: The Contemporaneity of Forgotten Jewish Thinkers*. Translated from the Spanish by Anne Day Dewey. Edited by John R. Welch. A volume in **Philosophy in Spain**

164.   Nancy Nyquist Potter, Editor, *Putting Peace into Practice: Evaluating Policy on Local and Global Levels*. A volume in **Philosophy of Peace**

165.   Matti Häyry, Tuija Takala, and Peter Herissone-Kelly, Editors, *Bioethics and Social Reality*. A volume in **Values in Bioethics**

166.   Maureen Sie, *Justifying Blame: Why Free Will Matters and Why it Does Not*. A volume in **Studies in Applied Ethics**

167.   Leszek Koczanowicz and Beth J. Singer, Editors, *Democracy and the Post-Totalitarian Experience*. A volume in **Studies in Pragmatism and Values**

168.   Michael W. Riley, *Plato's* Cratylus: *Argument, Form, and Structure*. A volume in **Studies in the History of Western Philosophy**

169.   Leon Pomeroy, *The New Science of Axiological Psychology*. Edited by Rem B. Edwards. A volume in **Hartman Institute Axiology Studies**

170.   Eric Wolf Fried, *Inwardness and Morality*

171.   Sami Pihlstrom, *Pragmatic Moral Realism: A Transcendental Defense.*
A volume in Studies in **Pragmatism and Values**

172.   Charles C. Hinkley II, *Moral Conflicts of Organ Retrieval: A Case for Constructive Pluralism.* A volume in **Values in Bioethics**

173.   Gábor Forrai and George Kampis, Editors, *Intentionality: Past and Future.* A volume in **Cognitive Science**

174.   Dixie Lee Harris, *Encounters in My Travels: Thoughts Along the Way.*
A volume in **Lived Values: Valued Lives**